THE BIG BOOK OF LOFTS
LE GRAND LIVRE DES LOFTS
DAS GROSSE LOFTBUCH

THE BIG BOOK OF LOFTS
LE GRAND LIVRE DES LOFTS
DAS GROSSE LOFTBUCH

EVERGREEN

EVERGREEN is an imprint of

Taschen GmbH

© 2005 TASCHEN GmbH

Hohenzollernring 53, D-50672 Köln

www.taschen.com

Editor Editrice Redakteur:
Simone Schleifer

French translation Traduction française Französische Übersetzung:
Marion Westerhoff

German translation Traduction alemande Deutsche Übersetzung:
Susanne Engler

English proof reading Relecture anglaise Korrektur lesen:
Matthew Clarke

Art director Direction artistique Art Direktor:
Mireia Casanovas Soley

Graphic design and layout Misse en page et maquette Graphische Gestaltung und Layout:
Diego González

ISBN: 3-8228-4182-X

Contents Index Inhalt

The origins of lofts can be traced back to the New York of the 1950s: at that time, artists and bohemians in search of cheap places to live and work began to move into abandoned late-nineteenth-century industrial buildings. These iron-framed premises were once the site of garment sweatshops, furniture companies, printmaker shops, warehouses, depositories, and factories. As industries moved away from Manhattan to cheaper areas, these buildings became vacant. Artists seized this low-cost opportunity to create a new American version of the Parisian artist's atelier and began moving into these spaces. As such, they unknowingly created what we now refer to as the loft.

Nowadays, the tendency to convert warehouses and factories into homes has extended everywhere, creating a style that can be applied to all types of spaces and inhabitants. What were once large, spartan shells, often occupied illegally by students and artists with limited financial means, have grown into elegant, luxurious residences reserved for a wealthy elite or premises for professionals who require a place in which they can both live and work. The common denominators are large, open areas with no dividing walls or partitions, floor-to-ceiling windows, and an extraordinary amount of natural light. Exposed materials from the original building – steel and wood, for example – allude to an industrial esthetic and a marriage between old and new adapted to the needs and tastes of the occupants. A recent (and flourishing) trend in loft design reflects a move away from transforming old factory buildings toward the conversion of conventional dwellings, using the loft approach to take advantage of their spatial and functional flexibility. New materials and design techniques have produced a generation of lofts that have become sophisticated and highly prized assets.

This book provides examples that illustrate how this trend is applied today, from huge industrial spaces to small premises where architects have to take the fullest possible advantage of the spatial possibilities to create a feeling of greater expansiveness. The ideas come from some of the most renowned architects in the world, and they can be applied to a variety of spaces and interpreted in different ways to suit personal tastes and satisfy specific requirements.

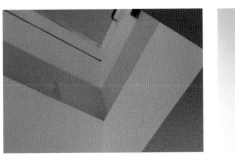
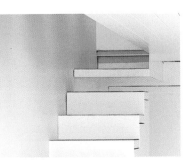

L'origine des lofts remonte au New York des années 50 : à cette époque, artistes et bohèmes en quête de logements et d'ateliers bon marché, commencèrent à s'installer dans des bâtiments industriels abandonnés de la fin du XIXe siècle. Autrefois, ces structures d'acier hébergeaient des ateliers de vêtement, des fabriques de meubles, des imprimeries, des entrepôts, des garde-meubles et des usines. Tous ces bâtiments furent délaissés lorsque les industries quittèrent Manhattan pour des quartiers moins chers. En s'installant dans ces locaux désaffectés très bon marché, les artistes profitèrent de cette véritable aubaine pour créer la version américaine des ateliers d'artistes parisiens. Sans le savoir, ils fondèrent ce que nous appelons aujourd'hui un loft.

De nos jours, la tendance à transformer entrepôts et usines en logement s'est généralisée un peu partout, créant un style adapté à un large éventail d'espaces et de personnes. Les grandes structures austères de jadis, souvent occupées de manière illégale par des étudiants et des artistes démunis, se sont métamorphosées en résidences élégantes et luxueuses, devenues l'apanage d'une élite aisée ou de professionnels en quête d'un lieu alliant domicile et bureau. Ces habitations ont de nombreuses caractéristiques communes : espaces ouverts sans murs ni cloisons, baies vitrées tout en hauteur et lumière du jour à profusion. La structure initiale apparente des bâtiments d'origine- mariant souvent l'acier et le bois- rappèle l'esthétique industrielle et l'alliance entre l'ancien et le moderne, adaptée aux besoins et goûts des occupants. La tendance récente (et florissante) du design de loft est en train de changer de cap : la restauration d'anciennes usines cède le pas à la reconversion de logements conventionnels, appliquant les critères de modulation de l'espace et des fonctions caractéristiques du loft. Les nouveaux matériaux et les récentes techniques de design ont engendré une nouvelle génération de lofts superbes, très en vogue.

Ce livre regorge d'exemples illustrant la tendance actuelle, dans un éventail allant d'immenses espaces industriels à de petits logements où les architectes ont optimisé les données spatiales pour exalter l'impression de largesse. Les idées présentées sont issues des plus prestigieux architectes du monde. Modulables selon les espaces, elles peuvent s'interpréter de mille et une façons, au gré des goûts et les besoins de chacun.

Die Ursprünge der Lofts liegen im New York der 50er Jahre: Damals begannen Künstler und Bohemians auf der Suche nach günstigen Räumen zum Wohnen und Arbeiten in verlassene Industriegebäude aus dem späten 19. Jahrhundert zu ziehen. Die Gebäude auf den von Eisenzäunen umgebenen Geländen beherbergten einst Textilmanufakturen, Möbelfabriken, Druckereien, Lagerhäuser, Depots und andere Betriebe. Seitdem die Betriebe nach und nach begonnen hatten, von Manhattan weg in billigere Zonen zu ziehen, standen die Gebäude leer. Künstler nutzten diese Gelegenheit und zogen in die kostengünstigen Gebäude, um eine amerikanische Version der typischen Pariser Ateliers zu kreieren. Damit schufen sie ohne es zu wissen, das was wir heute Loft nennen.

Heute ist der Trend, ehemalige Lagerhäuser und Fabrikgebäude in Wohnhäuser umzuwandeln, weit verbreitet und für alle Arten von Räumen und Bewohnern gültig. Was einst großflächige, spartanische Räume waren, oft illegal besetzt von Studenten und Künstlern mit begrenzten finanziellen Mitteln, sind heute elegante, luxuriöse Wohnungen, die einer wohlhabenden Elite vorbehalten sind, oder Wohn- und Arbeitsräume von gutverdienenden Freischaffenden. Geblieben sind die großen, offenen Bereiche ohne Mauern oder Trennwände, die hohen Fenster vom Boden bis zur Decke und die außergewöhnlich hohe Menge an natürlichem Licht. Offen liegende Baumaterialien der ursprünglichen Gebäude wie Stahl und Holz und sorgen für eine Industrieästhetik und einer Verbindung zwischen Alt und Neu, die zu den Anforderungen und dem Stil der neuen Bewohner passen. Ein neuer und florierender Trend beim Entwurf von Lofts geht weg von der Umwandlung alter Fabrikgebäude hin zur Neugestaltung von herkömmlichen Wohnungen, wobei die räumliche und funktionelle Flexibilität des Loftdesigns genutzt wird. Neue Materialien und Designverfahren haben eine neue Generation von ausgefeilten Lofts geschaffen, die zu hochgeschätzten Immobilienwerten geworden sind.

In diesem Buch werden Beispiele dargestellt, die zeigen, wie dieser Trend heute umgesetzt wird. Es werden riesige Industriegebäude vorgestellt und relativ kleine Räume gezeigt, bei denen die Architekten alle räumlichen Möglichkeiten bis ins Letzte ausnutzen mussten, um den Raum größer wirken zu lassen. Die Ideen zu den hier vorgestellten Lofts stammen von einigen der renommiertesten Architekten der Welt. Sie sind für eine Vielzahl von Gebäuden geeignet und können auf verschiedenen Weise interpretiert werden, um an stilistische und andere spezielle Anforderungen angepasst zu werden.

Structural Loft
Loft structural
Strukturelles Loft

Bergamo, Italy

Given the extraordinary height of the ceilings in this space, the architect decided to take advantage of the space and incorporate an additional level. The loft is articulated around thirteen steel posts scattered over the space in asymmetrical clusters. These posts support the system of horizontal planes to create a sensation of instability, arbitrarily piercing whatever comes in their way. The public zone was allocated to the lower level, while the private zones were lifted onto the upper structures. Two slanted posts puncture an oval glass dining table and continue through a floating structure with a bathroom suspended from the ceiling. The steel posts in the bedroom are both structural and decorative. Another key element is the intricate steel sculpture situated underneath a glass panel in the ground floor, which shines at night. The pervasive use of steel creates a distinctive style and a sense of continuity within the loft.

Dans cet espace, bénéficiant d'une hauteur de plafond extraordinaire, l'architecte a décidé d'optimiser l'espace en y incorporant un niveau supplémentaire. Le loft s'articule autour de treize piliers d'acier répartis dans l'espace en groupes asymétriques. Ils soutiennent le système de plans horizontaux afin de créer une sensation d'instabilité, traversant au hasard tout ce qui croise leur chemin. La zone publique est située au niveau inférieur tandis que les sphères privées sont élevées au niveau des structures supérieures. Deux piliers élancés crèvent une table de verre ovale et traversent ensuite une structure flottante dotée d'une salle de bains suspendue au plafond. Les colonnes d'aciers de la chambre à coucher sont structurales et décoratives. Une sculpture d'acier complexe, autre élément clé, se trouve sous un panneau de verre au rez-de-chaussée qui brille la nuit. L'omniprésence de l'acier crée un style particulier et imprime l'intérieur du sceau de la continuité.

Aufgrund der außergewöhnlichen Deckenhöhe baute der Architekt eine weitere Ebene ein. Das Loft wird von dreizehn, in asymetrischen Gruppen über den Raum verteilten Stahlpfosten gegliedert. Diese Pfosten stützen das System horizontaler Ebenen, das ein Gefühl von Instabilität entstehen lässt, und willkürlich alles durchsticht. Der öffentliche Bereich befindet sich unten, während die privaten Räume auf den oberen Strukturen liegen. Zwei schräge Postenstrukturen durchbohren einen Esstisch aus Glas und werden durch eine schwebende Struktur mit einem Badezimmer, die an der Decke hängt, weitergeführt. Die Stahlpfosten dienen im Schlafzimmer sowohl als Struktur- als auch als Dekorationselemente. Ein anderes Schlüsselelement ist die Stahlskulptur unter der Glasplatte im Erdgeschoss, die nachts beleuchtet ist. Das Vorherrschen des Materials Stahl schafft einen besonderen Stil und sorgt für Kontinuität in allen Räumen.

The use of glass to protect the catwalk ensures transparency and the flow of light throughout both levels of the loft.

L'emploi du verre, pour protéger la passerelle, dote l'espace de transparence et assure la fluidité de la lumière sur les deux niveaux du loft.

Durch den Einsatz von Glas zum Abschirmen des Stegs wurde große Transparenz erreicht, und das Tageslicht kann in beide Ebenen des Lofts eindringen.

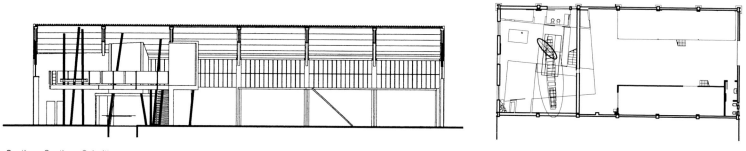

› Section Section Schnitt

› Plan Plan Grundriss

The intricate steel sculpture is another key element of the design. It shines at night and creates a distinctive effect, giving a sense of continuity within the loft.

Une sculpture d'acier complexe est aussi un élément clé de l'espace. Elle brille la nuit créant un effet particulier qui imprime l'intérieur du loft du sceau de la continuité.

Ein anderes Schlüsselelement dieses Projektes ist die ausgefallene Stahlstruktur. Nachts leuchtet sie und schafft eine einzigartige Atmosphäre innerhalb des Lofts.

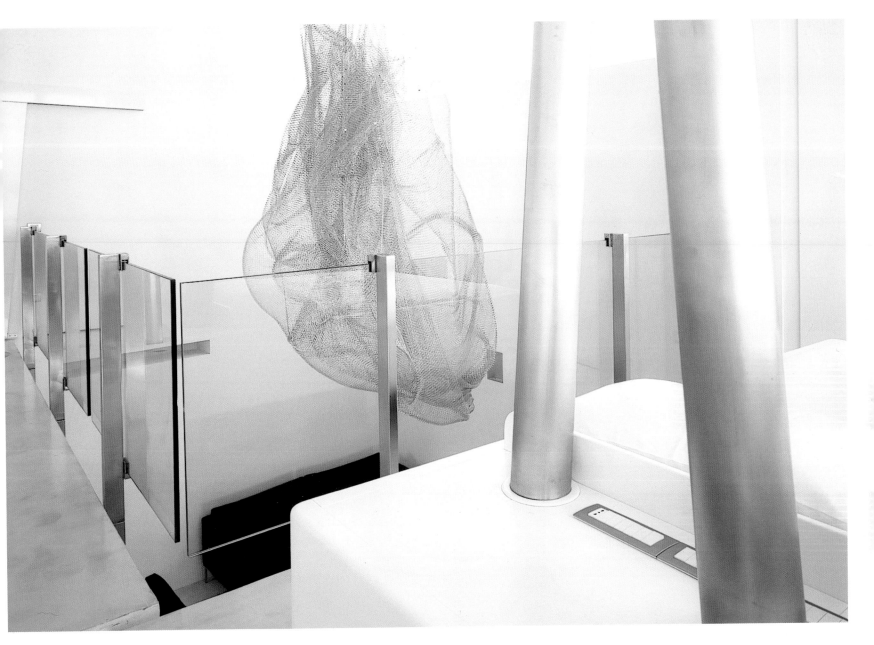

The steel pillars frame the bed from behind, serving as both structural and decorative elements.

Les piliers d'acier surplombent le lit et font à la fois partie de la structure et du décor.

Die Stahlpfosten, die direkt hinter dem Bett zusammenlaufen, haben sowohl eine strukturierende als auch eine dekorative Funktion.

The upper level consists of glass walkways that lead to the bedroom and bathroom.

Le niveau supérieur est constitué de passerelles de verre qui mènent à la salle de bains en marbre et à la chambre à coucher.

Die obere Etage besteht aus verglasten Stegen, die zum dem Marmorbadezimmer und dem Schlafzimmer fuehren.

Loft in A Coruña
Loft á A Coruña
Loft in A Coruña

A Coruña, Spain

A once dark and divided space was converted into a loft-style residence by tearing down the existing partitions and introducing a series of pivoting panels. The existing mezzanine was preserved and modified slightly around the staircase, while the hall was stripped to provide a greater sense of space in the entrance. The column that previously supported the mezzanine was replaced by a tension rod to relieve the perception of heaviness. Stairs recessed in the wall lead to an upper level that houses the bedroom, bathroom, and dressing room. The public areas and domestic functions are divided by small differences in levels or materials on the floor and ceiling. A translucent glass balcony subtly divides the two levels and provides privacy for the private areas. The furnishings, from the picture frames to the armchairs, were designed as a part of the project and include a complex kitchen module that contains all the appliances and bathroom elements.

Cet espace, autrefois sombre et cloisonné, est reconverti en une résidence style loft. Les parois sont remplacées par une série de panneaux pivotants. La mezzanine préexistante, conservée, est légèrement modifiée autour de l'escalier. Le hall d'entrée est mis à nu pour accroître la sensation d'espace. Dans un souci de légèreté, la colonne qui, au départ soutenait la mezzanine, est remplacée par un câble tenseur. L'escalier, encastré dans le mur, mène à l'étage supérieur, vers la chambre, la salle de bains et le dressing. La séparation entre les zones publiques et les zones privées est marquée par des différences de niveaux ou de matériaux de revêtement du sol et du plafond. Un balcon en verre transparent divise délicatement les deux niveaux, tout en assurant l'intimité des sphères privées. L'aménagement intérieur, allant des encadrements de tableaux aux fauteuils, à l'instar du module complexe de la cuisine entièrement équipée et dotée d'éléments de salle de bains.

Dieser ehemals dunkle und enge Raum wurde in eine Wohnung im Loftstil umgebaut. Dazu wurden Trennwände eingerissen und schwenkbare Paneelen konstruiert. Das Zwischengeschoss blieb erhalten und wurde im Treppenbereich leicht verändert. Der Flur wurde völlig geleert, um mehr Weite im Eingangsbereich zu schaffen. Die Säule wurde durch eine Zugstange ersetzt, die die Konstruktion leichter wirken lässt. Treppen in einer Wandnische führen zur oberen Ebene, wo sich Schlafzimmer, Bad und Ankleidezimmer befinden. Die öffentlichen Bereiche und häuslichen Funktionen sind durch leichte Höhenunterschiede oder verschiedene Decken- und Fußbodenmaterialien voneinander getrennt. Eine lichtdurchlässige Glasgalerie teilt die beiden Ebenen und sorgt für Privatsphäre. Der Entwurf der Möbel, von den Bilderrahmen bis zu den Sesseln, war Teil des Projektes. Dazu gehörten ein kompletten Küchenmodul mit allen Geräten und die Badezimmerelemente.

The furnishings were designed as a part of the architectural project and the stairs were recessed in the wall; they lead to an upper level that houses the bedroom, bathroom, and dressing room.

L'ameublement s'inscrit dans la conception du projet d'architecture et l'escalier, encastré dans le mur, mène à l'étage supérieur, vers la chambre, la salle de bains et le dressing.

Der Entwurf des Mobiliars war ein Teil des gesamten architektonischen Projektes. Die Treppe ist in einer Aussparung in der Wand untergebracht und führt in die obere Etage, in der sich das Schlafzimmer, Badezimmer und Ankleidezimmer befinden.

› Ground floor Rez-de-chaussée Erdgeschoss

› First floor Premier étage Erstes Obergeschoss

Gray Loft

New York, United States

The aim was to convert this loft on the eleventh floor of a building in the center of Manhattan into a home with three bedrooms, four bathrooms and a spacious living room suitable for large-scale social occasions. The design was preconditioned by the existence of two terraces and 23 windows distributed along three of the four façades, so it was decided that the layout would not break up this perimeter. So, the rooms are placed in the center of the home and are encircled by floating walls, providing an appearance of graceful lightness. The living room is an unbroken open space in which floor coverings and rugs mark off the different spaces for watching television, relaxing, listening to music or socializing with friends. The kitchen, made of stainless steel and corian, has been placed in the southeast corner, in order to take advantage of the morning sun.

L'idée était de convertir ce loft, situé au onzième étage d'un édifice, au centre de Manhattan, en un logement comportant trois chambres, quatre salles de bains et un salon spacieux pour de grandes réceptions. Le design devait tenir compte de l'existence de deux terrasses et de 23 fenêtres distribuées sur trois des quatre façades. Il fût donc décidé de garder ce périmètre. De ce fait, les pièces sont regroupées au cœur de l'habitation et entourées de murs flottants, conférant à l'ensemble une impression de gracieuse légèreté. Le salon est un espace totalement ouvert et fluide uniquement séparé par les tapis qui délimitent ainsi les différentes zones : télévision, détente, musique ou rencontre. Pour profiter du soleil matinal, la cuisine, en acier inoxydable et en Corian, a été installée dans l'angle sud-est.

Dieses Loft im elften Stockwerk eines Gebäudes im Zentrum von Manhattan sollte zu einer Wohnung mit drei Schlafzimmern, vier Badezimmern und einem großen Wohnzimmer umgebaut werden, in dem größere Zusammenkünfte möglich sind. Bei der Planung musste berücksichtigt werden, dass es zwei Terrassen und 23 Fenster an drei der vier Fassaden gab, die erhalten bleiben sollten. Deshalb wurden die Räume in die Mitte der Fabriketage gesetzt und von gleitenden Wänden umgeben, wodurch das Loft sehr hell wirkt. Das Wohnzimmer ist ein vollständig offener Raum, in dem der Fußbodenbelag und Teppiche die verschiedenen Bereiche zum Fernsehen, Entspannen, Musik hören oder mit Freunden reden markieren. Um von der Morgensonne zu profitieren, befindet sich die Küche aus Edelstahl im Südosten der Wohnung.

The large plasma-screen television is placed on a pivoting stand so that it can be conveniently turned and viewed from different points in the living room.

L'immense écran plasma de télévision, placé sur un socle pivotant, peut être dirigé au gré des besoins et vu à divers endroits du salon.

Der enorme Plasma-Fernseher befindet sich auf einem schwenkbaren Möbel, das in alle Richtungen des Wohnzimmers gedreht werden kann.

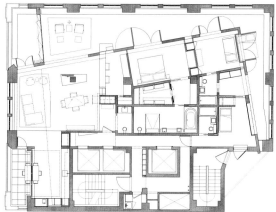

› Plan Plan Grundriss

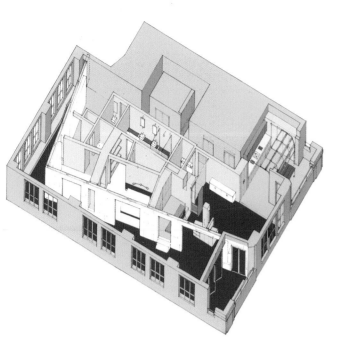

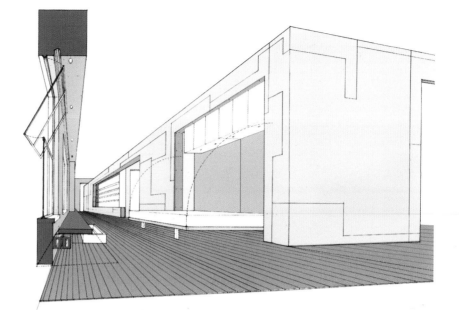

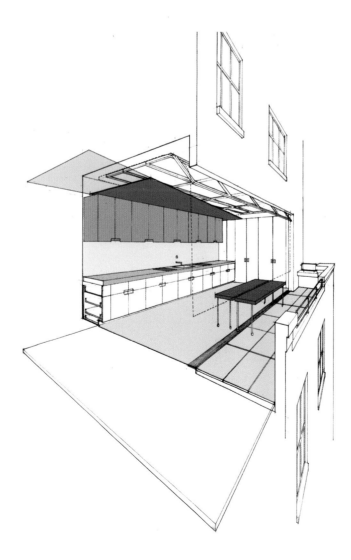

31

The leftover spaces, where the Corian wall approaches the façades, are used as dressing rooms, small storerooms, or makeshift guest rooms.

Les parties restantes, à l'endroit où le mur en Corian rejoint les façades, font office de dressing, de petits débarras ou de chambre d'amis improvisée.

Die übrigen Räume, in denen die mit Corian verkleideten Wände sich der Fassade annähern, werden als Ankleidezimmer, Abstellkammern oder behelfsmäßige Gästezimmer benutzt.

Loft A

Milan, Italy

This space was originally a traditional Milanese house with a balustrade, divided up into two small apartments, one on the top floor and the other on the bottom floor, connected to a spacious area which served as an art gallery. After a radical refurbishment, a spiral staircase was put in between the first and second floors, where the bedrooms are located. The rooms on the first floor have interior and exterior spaces and receive direct sunlight. They include the kitchen, which acts as a filter between the entrance and the rest of the house. The electrical system provides maximum flexibility in the lighting, which was a basic premise of the project. The architectural and structural concepts were largely determined by the materials used. Some structures are made of carbon fiber and whole swathes of the floor are covered with a resin. The original parquet floor was only retained in the bedroom.

Jadis une maison milanaise traditionnelle dotée d'un balcon, cet espace était divisé en deux petits appartements, un à l'étage supérieur et l'autre à l'étage inférieur, reliés à une large pièce servant de galerie d'art. Suite à une restauration d'envergure, un escalier en colimaçon a été installé entre les deux étages où se trouvent les chambres à coucher. Les pièces situées au premier étage, dotées d'espaces intérieur et extérieur, reçoivent la lumière du jour directe à l'instar de la cuisine qui sert de filtre entre l'entrée et le reste de la maison. Le système électrique permet un éclairage complètement modulable, idée directrice du projet. Les matériaux employés sont déterminants dans le concept architectural de l'ensemble. Certaines structures sont en fibres de carbone et dans son ensemble, le revêtement du sol est en résine. Seul le parquet de la chambre à coucher est d'origine.

Dieses Haus war einst ein traditionelles, mailändisches Gebäude mit Balustrade. Es wurde in zwei kleine Wohnungen im Ober- und Erdgeschoss aufgeteilt, die mit einer weitläufigen Kunstgalerie verbunden sind. Nach einer radikalen Sanierung wurde eine Wendeltreppe zwischen den ersten und zweiten Stockwerken eingebaut, wo sich die Schlafzimmer befinden. Die Räumlichkeiten der ersten Etage verfügen über innere und äußere Räume und erhalten direktes Sonnenlicht. Die Beleuchtung ist durch ein spezielles, elektrisches System sehr flexibel, was eine der Grundvoraussetzungen dieser Planung war. Die architektonischen und strukturellen Konzepte sind stark von den eingesetzten Materialien bestimmt. Manche Strukturen bestehen aus Kohlenstofffaser und stellenweise ist der Fußboden harzbeschichtet. Das Originalparkett ist nur noch im Schlafzimmer zu finden.

Natural light illuminates the lower floor and brightens up the corridor. The ramp of the stairs also receives sunshine thanks to the insertion of a window situated above it.

La lumière naturelle illumine l'étage inférieur et éclaire le couloir. La rampe des escaliers reçoit aussi les rayons de soleil grâce à une fenêtre insérée juste au-dessus.

Tageslicht dringt in das Untergeschoss und den Korridor. Auch die Treppe erhält durch ein oberes Fenster Licht von draußen.

The dining room is a spacious room characterized by functionality, while also providing open spaces for leisure to foster the social use of the room.

La salle à manger spacieuse se caractérise par sa fonctionnalité. Elle est également dotée d'espaces ouverts pour les loisirs, accentuant la fonction sociale de la pièce.

Das Esszimmer ist ein großer, funktioneller Raum, der sehr offen wirkt und als Treffpunkt dient.

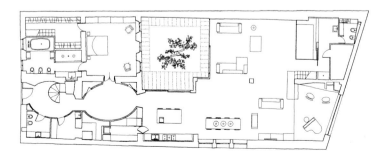

› Ground floor Rez-de-chaussée Erdgeschoss

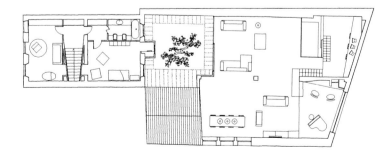

› First floor Premier étage Erstes Obergeschoss

e materials used are an important part of the architectural and structural concept. Some structures are made of carbon fiber and the flooring is covered with a resinous material.

choix des matériaux employés est un critère important du concept architectural et sculptural. Certaines structures sont en fibres de carbone et les sols sont recouverts de résines.

e benutzten Materialien sind ein wichtiger Bestandteil des architektonischen und strukturellen Konzeptes. Manche Strukturen bestehen aus Kohlenstofffasern, der Boden ist mit nem Material auf Harzgrundlage belegt.

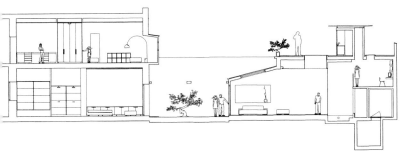

› Longitudinal section Section longitudinal Längsschnitt

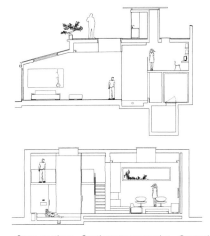

› Cross sections Sections transversales Querschnitte

43

Samarcanda stone is used in the design of the bathroom. It is part of the relaxation area and was designed to be integrated into the living-room area.

Le design de la salle de bains a été réalisé en pierre de Samarkand. Elle fait partie de la zone de relaxation. Sa conception l'intègre au salon.

Das Badezimmer ist mit dem Naturstein Samarcanda gestaltet. Es gehört zur Entspannungszone und ist so angelegt, dass es in den Wohnbereich integriert ist.

oston, United States

Hunter Ritaco Loft

The owners assigned Ruhl Walker Architects to esign the complete interior of their residential loft nd they desired total openness and flexibility, ith all the spaces flowing together as freely as ossible with multiple domestic, socializing and usiness functions. The pre-existing, long, winowless side walls are activated by modulations of e new ceiling planes and custom millwork on ne side, and a virtual 'floating window' of steel nd translucent, back-lit acrylic on the other. This anslucent wall, the loft's main source of light, pens up to become a home office at one end and onceals the dressing room at the other. Large oncealed sliding doors allow the owners to econfigure the spaces to accommodate constant- fluctuating needs for privacy. The flooring is harcoal-gray stained maple in the main spaces, oned green limestone in the master bathroom, nd black slate in the entrance and guest bathoom.

Les propriétaires ont chargé le bureau d'études Ruhl Walker Architects du design de tout l'intérieur de leur loft résidentiel, selon les critères spatiaux suivants : ouverture totale, flexibilité, fluidité, liberté maximale et fonctions multiples - domestiques, sociales et professionnelles. Les longs murs latéraux préexistants, dépourvus de fenêtres, sont activés par de nouveaux plafonds en panneaux modulables et un mécanisme d'engrenage sur un côté. Une « fenêtre flottante » virtuelle en acier et acrylique translucide rétro-éclairé s'inscrit de l'autre côté. Ce mur translucide, source de lumière principal, s'ouvre et se métamorphose, d'un côté, en bureau, et de l'autre, dissimule le dressing. Grâce à de grandes portes coulissantes intégrées, le propriétaire peut reconfigurer l'espace au gré de ses besoins d'intimité. Le sol des espaces principaux est en érable ponctué de gris charbon, en grés vert vif dans la salle de bains du maître et en ardoise noire dans l'entrée et la salle de bains des amis.

Die Kunden beauftragten Ruhl Walker Architects mit dem Entwurf des gesamten Lofts. Sie wünschten sich offene Räume, die sowohl sozialen als auch geschäftlichen Funktionen dienen. Die bereits vorhandenen, fensterlosen Seitenwände wurden durch Modulationen der neuen Deckenplatten und Holzfertigplatten auf einer Seite und dem virtuellen „schwebenden Fenster" aus Stahl und lichtdurchlässigen, von hinten beleuchteten Acryl auf der anderen Seite belebt. Die lichtdurchlässige Wand und Hauptlichtquelle öffnet sich zu einem Heimbüro auf der einen Seite und verbirgt das Ankleidezimmer auf der anderen Seite. Große, verdeckte Schiebetüren machen es möglich, die Räume zu verändern und die jeweils gewünschte Privatsphäre zu schaffen. Der Fußboden ist in den Haupträumen mit dunkelgrauem Ahorn und im Hauptbadezimmer mit grünem, polierten Kalkstein belegt. Im Eingangsbereich und den Gästebadezimmern findet man schwarzen Schiefer.

The owners desired total openness and flexibility, combined with a range of materials that would enhance these general aims and stimulate the senses.

Les propriétaires voulaient une ouverture et flexibilité totales, alliées à un éventail de matériaux renforçant cet objectif et stimulant les sens .

Der Eigentümer wünschte sich eine offene und veränderbare Umgebung, kombiniert mit einer Vielzahl von Materialien, die diese Wirkung noch unterstreichen und die Sinne anrege

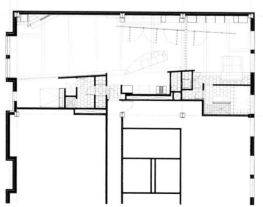

› Plan Plan Grundriss

...arge, concealed sliding doors allow the owners to reconfigure the spaces to accommodate the constantly fluctuating needs for privacy.

...e grandes portes coulissantes escamotables permettent aux maîtres des lieux de remodeler l'espace au gré des fluctuations de leur besoin d'intimité.

...roße, verdeckte Schiebetüren machen es möglich, die Räume zu verändern und die jeweils gewünschte Privatsphäre zu schaffen.

Multimedia Studio
Studio multimédia
Multimediastudio

Barcelona, Spain

The loft was created for a multimedia artist whose colorful works are design elements that bring vitality to the space. The interior designers' philosophy springs from their perception of minimalism as a series of concepts that value simplicity, austerity, and elegance, rather than a passing aesthetic trend. The kitchen became the center of attention; a free-standing island with a stainless steel countertop faces the living area, flanked by a wall of closets. A partition conceals the bedroom and stops short of the ceiling to favor the entrance of light. In the bedroom, an original sculpture serves as a decorative and practical coat hanger. The bathroom is set behind a half-height stone wall that does not obscure the high windows and the structural columns, while the light materials used inside contrast with these solid structures. The counter seems to float between the two columns, while the glass basin rests lightly on top of it.

Le loft a été créé pour un artiste du multimédia dont les œuvres de design colorées ravivent l'espace. La philosophie du designer est de percevoir le minimalisme davantage comme une série de concepts valorisant la simplicité, la sobriété et l'élégance plutôt qu'une tendance esthétique éphémère. La cuisine centralise l'attention : un îlot unique recouvert d'inox fait face au salon, flanqué d'un mur de placards. Une cloison masque la chambre à coucher et s'arrête peu avant le plafond pour laisser passer la lumière. Dans la chambre à coucher, une sculpture originale décorative et pratique à la fois, fait office de portemanteaux. La salle de bains se love derrière un mur de pierre à mi-hauteur, laissant ainsi filtrer la lumière des fenêtres hautes sans pour autant cacher les colonnes structurales. Les matériaux légers de l'intérieur contrastent avec ces structures solides. Le plan de toilette semble flotter entre les deux colonnes avec l'évier de verre posé délicatement dessus.

Dieses Loft wurde für einen Multimediakünstler geschaffen, dessen bunten Arbeiten die Räume beleben. Grundlage der Gestaltung war ein minimalistisches Konzept, das auf Werten wie Einfachheit, Nüchternheit und Eleganz beruht, und kein vorübergehender, ästhetischer Trend ist. Die Küche bildet in diesem Loft den Mittelpunkt, eine freistehende Insel, die dem Wohnbereich, begrenzt von einer Wand voller Wandschränke, gegenüber liegt. Ein Raumteiler, der nicht ganz bis zur Decke reicht, so dass noch Licht einfällt, trennt das Schlafzimmer ab. Im Schlafzimmer dient eine originelle Skulptur als dekorativer und praktischer Kleiderständer. Das Badezimmer befindet sich hinter einer halbhohen Steinmauer, die die hohen Fenster und Säulen nicht verdeckt. Die leichten Materialien im Badezimmer bilden einen Gegensatz zu diesen festen Strukturen. Der Waschtisch, auf den sich ein leichtes, gläsernes Waschbecken stützt, scheint zwischen zwei Säulen zu schweben.

The loft was created for a multimedia artist whose colorful works endow the space with life.

Le loft a été créé pour un artiste du multimédia dont les œuvres de design, hautes en couleur, ravivent l'espace.

Das Loft wurde für einen Multimediakünstler dekoriert, dessen bunten Werke es mit Leben füllen.

The kitchen became the center of attention; a free-standing island with a stainless steel countertop faces the living area, which is flanked by a wall covered with closets.

La cuisine monopolise l'attention : un îlot central doté d'un comptoir en inox fait face au salon, flanqué d'un mur de placards intégrés.

In diesem Loft bildet die Küche den Mittelpunkt, der dem Wohnbereich, begrenzt von einer Wand voller Wandschränke, gegenüber liegt.

the bedroom, an original sculpture serves as a decorative but practical coat hanger. A partition conceals the bedroom and stops short of the ceiling to enhance the entrance of light.

ans la chambre à coucher, une sculpture originale, décorative et pratique à la fois, fait office de porte manteaux. Une cloison masque la chambre et s'arrête peu avant le plafond

ur laisser filtrer la lumière.

Schlafzimmer dient eine originelle Skulptur als dekorativer und praktischer Kleiderständer. Ein Raumteiler, der nicht ganz bis zur Decke reicht, damit noch Licht einfällt, trennt das

chlafzimmer ab.

ht materials like wood and glass were used in the bathroom, which is situated behind a half-height stone wall and preserves the view of the tall windows and the structural columns.

s matériaux légers, à l'instar du verre sont utilisés dans la salle de bains, située derrière un mur de pierre à mi-hauteur, préservant la vue sur les hautes fenêtres et les colonnes ucturales.

Badezimmer wurden leichte Materialien wie Holz und Glas benutzt. Es liegt hinter einer halbhohen Steinmauer und man sieht von dort aus noch die großen Fenster und die Säu- der Struktur.

Loft in Milan
Loft à Milan
Loft in Milan

Milan, Italy

Formerly a carpenter's workshop, these premises were transformed into a living space for a couple of young graphic designers and their child. The loft is characterized by high ceilings that consist on one side of wooden beams and on the other of metal sheets. The architect chose to divide the vertical space into two and insert a mezzanine level, accessed by a steel and wood staircase, which leads to the studio (slightly taller than the remaining space). The pitched glass ceiling was layered with bamboo screens and draped with white fabric to diffuse the direct sunlight, which, in turn, is filtered through two glass floor into the dining room area directly below. Downstairs, the living space looks onto the bright orange kitchen and dining area that contrasts strikingly with the antique table and chairs. The decoration in the child's bedroom was created by her mother and creates an atmosphere of magic and fantasy.

Atelier de charpentier par le passé, cet endroit a été transformé en un espace de vie pour un couple de jeunes graphistes et leur enfant. Ce loft se distingue par de hauts plafonds parés d'un côté de poutres de bois et de l'autre, de plaques de métal. L'architecte a pris le parti de diviser l'espace vertical en deux et d'y intégrer une mezzanine reliée par un escalier d'acier et de bois menant au studio (légèrement surélevé par rapport au reste de l'espace). Le haut plafond de verre est habillé de paravents en bambous et drapés de tissu diffusant la lumière directe du soleil, filtrée, tour à tour, par deux sols en verre, dans l'espace de la salle à manger située juste en dessous. En bas, le salon donne directement sur la cuisine et la salle à manger orange vif, contrastant ainsi avec les chaises et la table anciennes. La décoration de la chambre d'enfant, empreinte de magie et de fantaisie, est l'œuvre de la mère.

Diese einstige Schreinerwerkstatt wurde in ein lebendiges Zuhause für ein Paar, beide Grafikdesigner, und deren Kind umgestaltet. Das Loft hat hohe Decken, die auf einer Seite aus Holzbalken und auf der anderen aus Metallplatten besteht. Der Architekt beschloss, den vertikalen Raum in zwei Bereiche zu unterteilen und ein Zwischengeschoss einzuziehen, das man über eine Treppe aus Stahl und Holz erreicht. Diese führt ins Atelier (etwas größer als der restliche Raum). Die geneigte Glasdecke ist mit Bambusrahmen und weißem Stoff bedeckt, um das direkte Sonnenlicht zu zerstreuen, das dann durch die beiden Glasfußböden bis in den Essbereich direkt darunter dringt. Unten liegt der Wohnbereich der hellorangenen Küche und dem Essbereich gegenüber, die in einem starken Kontrast zu dem antiken Tisch und Stühlen stehen. Die magische und phantastische Atmosphäre des Kinderzimmers entstand durch die Dekoration, die die Mutter selbst entworfen hat.

The metal structure incorporates a table-like surface that helps to accentuate the unity of the two levels.

La structure en métal comprend une surface plane qui permet de souligner l'unité entre les deux niveaux.

In der Metallstruktur ist eine Oberfläche enthalten, die einem Tisch gleicht und eine Verbindung zwischen den beiden Ebenen herstellt.

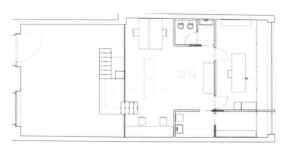

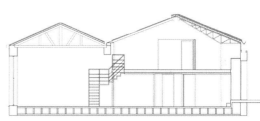

› **Ground floor** Rez-de-chaussée Erdgeschoss

› **First floor** Premier étage Erstes Obergeschoss

› **Section** Section Schnitt

ect sunlight is filtered into the dining room area directly below through two glass panels in the floor.

lumière directe du jour est filtrée vers la salle à manger en dessous par deux panneaux de verre dans le sol.

rch die beiden Glasplatten im Fußboden filtert sich direktes Sonnenlicht in das Speisezimmer direkt darunter.

...nadian pine covers most of the floor, although there are traces of marble in the entrance, kitchen and bathroom.

...plupart des sols sont recouverts de pin canadien, bien que le marbre ponctue l'entrée, la cuisine et la salle de bains.

...r größte Teil des Bodens ist mit dem Holz der Kanadischen Hemlocktanne belegt. Im Eingangsbereich, in der Küche und im Badezimmer ist der Bodenbelag teilweise aus Marmor.

Park Avenue Loft

New York, United States

To construct this loft, the existing interior was gutted and the bare space was taken as the starting point for the renovation. Acid-etched glass, the most important material present, was used to create divisions that optimize the circulation of light. The concept was developed around an open, sky-lit kitchen designed as a free-standing island within the living area to enhance the feeling of spaciousness. Furthermore, daylight was required to penetrate all the areas in the loft. To achieve this, no single wall reaches the ceiling, and a select few are surrounded by glass. The two large walls at either end of the living room, framed from behind by the acid-etched glass panels, mark the passageway into the private areas and act as an attractive backdrop for paintings and other objects. Closets were integrated into the perimeter windowsills to provide extra storage, and their wide surface also doubles as additional seating for social occasions.

Ce loft est le fruit de la rénovation d'un espace intérieur vide et dépouillé. Le recours au verre gravé à l'acide, matériau omniprésent dans ce projet, a permis de réaliser un système de partition optimalisant la circulation de la lumière. Le concept architectural a été développé autour d'un bloc cuisine ouvert et lumineux, posé à l'instar d'un îlot, au cœur de la salle de séjour, pour rehausser la sensation d'espace. En outre, toutes les zones du loft devant recevoir la lumière du jour, aucun mur ne touche le plafond et seuls quelques-uns uns sont gainés de verre. Deux murs situés à chaque extrémité du salon, encadrés à l'arrière par des panneaux en verre gravés à l'acide, marquent le passage vers les sphères privées et servent de support original pour tableaux ou autres objets. La superficie étendue du périmètre des rebords de fenêtres permet d'y intégrer des armoires offrant un supplément de rangement et de doubler le nombre de places assises lors de réceptions.

Um dieses Loft zu bauen, wurde die existierende Struktur vollständig geleert und als Ausgangspunkt für die Renovierung benutzt. Hauptsächlich wurde geätztes Glas eingesetzt, damit wurden Raumteiler geschaffen, die Licht durchlassen. Der Mittelpunkt des Raums ist eine offene Küche mit Dachfenster, die eine freistehende Insel im Wohnbereich bildet und so das Gefühl von Weite noch verstärkt. Außerdem sollte Tageslicht in alle Winkel gelangen. Deshalb reicht keine Wand bis zur Decke, und einige der Wände sind von Glas umgeben. Die beiden großen Seitenwände des Wohnzimmers, die von hinten mit geätzten Glaspaneelen versehen sind, markieren den Übergang zu den privateren Räumen und bilden einen attraktiven Hintergrund für Gemälde und andere Objekte. In den Fensterbänken wurden Wandschränke untergebracht, um zusätzlichen Platz zu schaffen, und die Fensterbänke dienen auch als zusätzliche Sitzgelegenheit.

The concept was developed around an open, sky-lit kitchen designed as a free-standing island within the living area to enhance the feeling of spaciousness.

Le concept architectural évolue autour du bloc cuisine ouvert et lumineux, posé à l'instar d'un îlot au cœur de la salle de séjour pour rehausser la sensation d'espace.

Ausgangspunkt des Konzeptes war die offene Küche mit Dachfenster, die wie eine freistehende Insel mitten im Wohnbereich liegt, was das Gefühl von Offenheit und viel Platz noch verstärkt.

70

One of the main objectives of the design was to allow daylight to penetrate all the areas of the loft, thus brightening up the dark wood on the floors and in the kitchen.

L'idée essentielle qui anime le design est de laisser entrer la lumière dans toutes les zones du loft, éclaircissant ainsi le bois sombre des sols et de la cuisine.

Eines der Hauptziele dieses Projektes war es, das Tageslicht in alle Zonen des Lofts dringen zu lassen, und so das dunkle Holz der Fußböden und der Küche heller wirken zu lassen.

› Plan Plan Grundriss

Glass Bridge
Passerelle de verre
Glasbrücke

lew York, United States

A complete renovation of these premises led to ⸱e creation of a generous, two-story space ⸱esigned to adapt to a young couple with chil-⸱ren. The main volume is delineated by full-height ⸱alls on three sides and carried across the fourth ⸱de by the glass and aluminum mezzanine rail-⸱gs and the overhanging upper-level bedroom. ⸱ne kitchen and dining area, media room, and ⸱ridge are configured as secondary volumes ⸱eathed in translucent glass. On the mezzanine ⸱vel, the floor joining the media room to the chil-⸱ren's bedrooms takes the form of a laminated-⸱lass bridge passing over the dining area. To ⸱low the private rooms to receive light and con-⸱ect with the living space, the partitions separat-⸱g them were fashioned from etched-glass pan-⸱s framed in aluminum and made with hinged ⸱aves. The materials are treated as the surfaces ⸱f concave spaces and volume is explored as an ⸱chitectural space rather than a sculptural form.

Entièrement restauré, ce lieu s'est converti en un loft spacieux sur deux niveaux, pour un jeune couple avec enfants. Le volume principal, délimité par des murs tout en hauteur sur trois côtés, s'élance vers le quatrième côté grâce à la grille de verre et d'aluminium de la mezzanine et à la chambre suspendue du niveau supérieur. La cuisine et la salle à manger, la pièce réservée à la télévision et au bridge sont configurées comme des volumes secondaires gainés de verre translucide. Au niveau de la mezzanine, le sol reliant la salle de télévision aux chambres d'enfants, se transforme en passe-relle de verre feuilleté, enjambant la salle à manger. Les cloisons sont en panneaux de verre gravé, encadrés d'aluminium, parés d'inclusions de feuilles pour accroître la lumière dans les chamb-res privées et les relier à la pièce à vivre. Les maté-riaux sont traités comme des surfaces d'espaces concaves. Dans l'étude des volumes, l'architecture de l'espace prime sur la forme sculpturale.

Durch den Umbau dieses Gebäudes entstand ein großzügiger, zweistöckiger Raum für ein jun-ges Paar mit Kindern. Das Hauptvolumen wird auf drei Seiten von deckenhohen Wänden begrenzt, auf der vierten Seite von dem Geländer des Zwi-schengeschosses aus Glas und Aluminium und dem hervorstehendem Schlafzimmer im oberen Stockwerk. Der Küchen- und Essbereich, das Medienzimmer und die Brücke bilden mit Glas verkleidete, sekundäre Volumen. Auf dem Zwi-schengeschoss wird der Flur, der das Medienzim-mer mit dem Kinderzimmer verbindet, zu einer verkleideten Glasbrücke über das Esszimmer. Damit Tageslicht in die privaten Zimmer fällt und diese mit dem Wohnbereich verbunden bleiben, bestehen die Raumteiler aus geätzten Glasschei-ben mit Aluminiumrahmen und Flügeln mit Schar-nieren. Die Materialien werden wie Oberflächen konkaver Räume behandelt.

The white columns and the wooden flooring create a welcome contrast to the glass and aluminum railings on the mezzanine.

Les colonnes blanches et le sol boisé créent un beau contraste avec le verre et l'aluminium de la balustrade de la mezzanine.

Die weißen Säulen und der Holzfußboden schaffen einen willkommenen Kontrast zu den Glas- und Aluminiumschienen des Zwischengeschosses.

› First floor Premier étage Erstes Obergeschoss   › Ground floor Rez-de-chaussée Erdgeschoss

The floor that connects the media room to the children's bedrooms was constructed of laminated glass and configured as a bridge passing over the dining area.

...e sol, reliant la salle de télévision aux chambres d'enfants, se transforme en passerelle de verre feuilleté qui enjambe la salle à manger.

...er Fußboden, der den Medienraum mit dem Kinderschlafzimmer verbindet, besteht aus beschichteten Glas und bildet eine Brücke, die über das Speisezimmer führt.

New York, United States

Wall Street Loft

In 1995, New York's City Hall encouraged contractors to convert empty office buildings in lower Manhattan into homes. The real estate group Time Equities took advantage of the proposal and hired the architectural team Chroma AD to remodel a six-story building into 13 lofts. The dramatic shadows and piercing rays of natural light found in this area were the conceptual inspiration for this project. By creating luminous white boxes and punctuating them with black elements, the architects hoped to reflect the feel of Wall Street. Wall-to-wall windows and enormous ceilings take advantage of all available daylight. Highly reflective epoxy-resin floors bounce light throughout the loft with the monolithic black kitchen. The removal of false ceilings allowed the concrete beams to be exposed for the first time. The kitchen, bathrooms, and open spaces were drawn up to harmonize with the pre-existing beams and columns.

En 1995, le City Hall de New York a encouragé les constructeurs à convertir en logements les bureaux vides situés dans le bas Manhattan. Le groupe immobilier Time Equities a répondu à l'offre et a chargé le cabinet d'architectes Chroma AD de remodeler un immeuble de six étages en 13 lofts. La conception du projet s'est inspirée du jeu d'ombre et de lumière naturelle théâtral qui règne dans ce quartier. Par le biais de boites blanches lumineuses, ponctuées d'éléments noirs, les architectes ont essayé de reproduire l'ambiance de Wall Street. D'énormes fenêtres et d'immenses plafonds absorbent toute la lumière du jour possible. Des sols en résine époxy reflètent la lumière et la renvoient dans tout le loft, doté d'une cuisine monolithique noire. Le retrait des faux plafonds a permis de découvrir pour la première fois les poutres en béton. La cuisine, les salles de bains et les espaces de vie sont conçus pour s'intégrer harmonieusement aux poutres et colonnes préexistantes.

Im Jahr 1995 ermutigte die Stadtverwaltung von New York die Bauunternehmer dazu, Bürogebäude in Lower Manhattan in Wohnungen umzugestalten. Die Immobiliengruppe Time Equities nutzte dieses Angebot aus und nahm das Architektenteam Chroma AD unter Vertrag, um ein sechsstöckiges Gebäude in 13 Lofts umzubauen. Das Spiel aus Schatten und grellem Licht in diesem Bezirk diente den Planern als konzeptuelle Inspiration. Sie gestalteten helle, weiße Kästen mit gezielt eingesetzten, schwarzen Elementen, um so das Gefühl von Wall Street zu reflektieren. Durch die Wände, einnehmenden Fenster und hohen Decken dringt reichlich Tageslicht. Reflektierende, mit Epoxidharz beschichtete Böden werfen das Licht durch das Loft einschließlich der schwarzen Küche. Die falschen Decken wurden entfernt und die Betonbalken sichtbar gemacht. Die Küche, das Bad und die offenen Räume harmonieren mit den alten Balken und Säulen.

The wall-to-ceiling windows bath the dining room with light during the day, while highly reflective epoxy-resin floors bounce light throughout the loft.

Les baies vitrées baignent la pièce de lumière naturelle pendant la journée, renvoyée par les sols en résine époxy dans tout le loft.

Tagsüber fällt durch die bis zur Decke reichenden Fenster sehr viel Licht, das von den reflektierenden, mit Epoxidharz beschichteten Fußböden durch das ganze Loft zurückgeworfen w

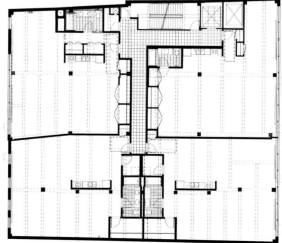

› Plan Plan Grundriss

By creating bright, white boxes and punctuating them with black elements, the architects hoped to reflect the feel of Wall Street.

En créant de larges boites blanches, émaillées d'éléments noirs, l'architecte a tenté de recréer l'ambiance de Wall Street.

Der Architekt gestaltete helle, weiße Kästen mit gezielt eingesetzten, schwarzen Elementen, um so ein Gefühl von Wall Street entstehen zu lassen.

Transformable Loft
Loft modulable
Veränderbares Loft

ome, Italy

This loft, located in Rome, Italy, consists of two eas: a large rectangular space flanked by a wall windows and another with glass doors that en onto a private terrace. The areas are divided a sequence of pillars and panels. Two large iding panels screen off the living and dining eas from the entrance, while a set of hinged nels fold out to close off one area so that it can e used as a guest bedroom. These folding pan- s reduce to the width of the pillar, leaving the liv- g space completely open. A suspended blue all and a stone platform into which the mattress inserted delineate the bedroom. In the kitchen, e black granite countertop extends beyond the tchen module to serve as a bar or breakfast ble. In the bathroom, the same intense blue ed as a backdrop to the bedroom covers the ors.

Ce loft, situé à Rome, en Italie, offre deux espaces : l'un est un large rectangle flanqué d'un mur de fenêtres et l'autre est doté de portes en verre qui s'ouvrent sur une terrasse privée. Une série de colonnes et de panneaux scandent l'espace. Deux cloisons coulissantes séparent le salon et la salle à manger de l'entrée et une série de partitions se déplient pour clore l'espace et créer une chambre d'invités. Ces panneaux réduits à la taille d'une colonne, créent un espace de vie totalement ouvert. Un mur bleu suspendu et une plateforme en pierre dotée d'un matelas intégré définissent la chambre à coucher. Dans la cuisine, le plan de travail en granit noir prolonge le module de la cuisine et sert de bar ou de table pour le petit-déjeuner. Le sol de la salle de bains est revêtu du même bleu intense utilisé en toile de fond pour la chambre.

Dieses Loft in Rom besteht aus zwei Bereichen: ein großer, rechteckiger Raum begrenzt von einer Fensterwand und ein Anderer mit Glastüren, die zur privaten Terrasse führen. Die verschiedenen Bereiche sind durch Pfeiler und Tafeln unterteilt. Zwei große Gleitpaneele schirmen den Wohn- und Essbereich vom Eingang ab, während eine Reihe von gefalteten Paneelen auseinandergezogen werden können, um ein Gästezimmer abzuteilen. Diese zusammenfaltbaren Paneele reduzieren die Breite des Pfeilers und lassen den Wohnbereich völlig offen. Eine hängende, blaue Wand und eine Steinplattform, in der die Matratze eingelassen ist, begrenzen das Schlafzimmer. In der Küche geht die Arbeitsfläche aus schwarzen Granit über das Küchenmodul hinaus und dient als Bar und Frühstückstisch. Im Badezimmer findet man das gleiche, intensive Blau des Schlafzimmers im Fußboden.

The parquet floor, white walls, and soft colors of the furniture create a warm atmosphere throughout the living room.

Le parquet, les murs blancs et les couleurs douces des meubles, imprégnent tout le salon d'une atmosphère chaude.

Durch den Parkettboden, die weißen Wände und die Möbel in sanften Farben herrscht im ganzen Wohnzimmer eine warme Atmosphäre.

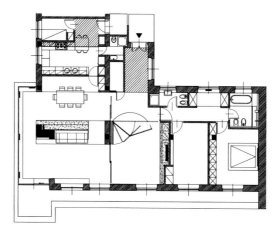

› Plan Plan Grundriss

e black granite countertop extends beyond the kitchen module to serve as a bar or breakfast table.

plan de travail, en granit noir, prolonge le module de la cuisine et sert de bar ou de table pour le petit déjeuner.

e Arbeitsfläche aus schwarzem Granit reicht über das Küchenmodul hinaus, und dient so auch als Bar oder Frühstückstisch.

e floor in the bathroom displays the same bright blue color that is used as a backdrop for the bedroom.

sol de la salle de bains est revêtu du même bleu intense utilisé en toile de fond pour la chambre.

r Boden im Badezimmer ist im gleichen Hellblau gehalten, das auch als Hintergrundfarbe für das Schlafzimmer dient.

Attic in Vienna
Attique à Vienne
Dachgeschoss in Wien

enna, Austria

The main concerns in residential architecture are nctional or esthetic but Lichtblau & Wagner have roduced energy-saving concepts into this field. achieve greater efficiency, these young Austrian chitects have ruled out superficial luxuries like arble bathrooms, pointless terraces, and andiose entrances to concentrate on a flexible oject that economizes on energy, expense, and ace. Four basic, 530-sq. ft units were conceived. ey are organized in pairs, with an additional ace that may be added to one apartment or the her. This alteration is easy to achieve by simply locating partitions. The communal spaces con-in a storeroom, a laundry, and a multipurpose ea for meetings or parties (offsetting the lack of ace in the studios). Positions have been suggest-d for the kitchen and bathroom but they can be oved without any building work. The clients can arrange their home according to their tastes or quirements.

L'architecture d'habitation a pour principes essentiels, le fonctionnel ou l'esthétique. Mais Lichtblau & Wagner y a ajouté le concept d'écono-mie d'énergie. Pour plus d'efficacité, ces jeunes architectes autrichiens ont éliminé le luxe superfi-ciel, comme les salles de bains en marbre, les ter-rasses inutiles et les halls d'entrée grandioses pour se consacrer à des projets modulables, offrant un gain d'énergie, de coût et d'espace. Ils ont conçu quatre unités de base de 50 m², organi-sées par paire et dotées d'un espace supplémen-taire que l'on peut ajouter à un appartement ou à un autre. Ces modifications sont facilitées par des cloisons modulables. L'espace commun abrite un coin rangement, une laverie et une zone polyva-lente pour les réunions ou les fêtes (compensant le manque d'espace dans les studios). Les empla-cements pour la cuisine et les salles de bains sont prévus mais sont modifiables. Les clients peuvent réaménager leur intérieur selon leurs besoins.

In der Wohnungsarchitektur wird meist der Schwerpunkt auf Funktionalität und Ästhetik gelegt. Lichtblau & Wagner legen ebenso großen Wert auf energiesparendes Bauen. Dazu verzich-ten diese jungen österreichischen Architekten auf oberflächlichen Luxus wie Marmorbadezimmer, unnütze Terrassen und grandiose Eingangsberei-che und konzentrieren sich auf eine flexible Pla-nung, bei der Energie, Kosten und Raum gespart werden. Es wurden vier 50 m² große Basiseinhei-ten entworfen, paarweise organisiert. Es existiert ein zusätzlicher Raum, der sehr einfach einer der beiden Wohnungen hinzugefügt werden kann, indem die Raumteiler umplatziert werden. Es gibt einen gemeinsamen Lagerraum, einen Wäsche-raum und einen Vielzweckbereich, in dem gefei-ert werden kann (um den Platzmangel auszuglei-chen). Die Lage der Küchen und Badezimmer können verändert werden, und das Haus nach eigenem Wunsch gestalten werden.

The space beneath the sliding windows may be used as a terrace, gallery, or greenhouse. Drapes separate this space from the rest of the home, creating a sensation of warmth an comfort.

L'espace en dessous des baies vitrées coulissantes peut servir de terrasse, de galerie ou de serre. Il est séparé du reste de la maison par des tentures, créant une sensation de chale et de confort.

Der Raum unterhalb der Schiebefenster kann als Terrasse, Galerie oder Wintergarten benutzt werden. Dieser Raum ist durch Vorhänge vom Rest des Hauses abgetrennt. Er wirkt war und komfortabel.

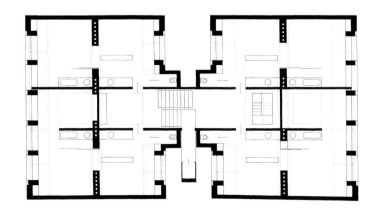

› Plan Plan Grundriss

Loft on Rue Popincourt
Loft de la rue Popincourt
Loft in der Rue Popincourt

aris, France

This loft, in which an old structure coexists with a odern architectural approach, was configured as space in which natural light is omnipresent. This oject, a radical intervention in a practically empty ace, was based on two premises: on the one nd, the preservation of the façades and the roofs d, on the other, a new construction in the center the home, once occupied by the coach house. e architect took advantage not only of the exist- g structure but also the back patio, now a garden, nich provides all the bedrooms with light and a nse of spaciousness. Furthermore, the respect r the design of the original façade allows the ilding to blend in with the neighboring buildings. e lobby leads to the sitting room, which is a rge space flooded with light that gives on to the tio. The filters of light are a line of bamboo in e patio and screens made of translucent poly- rbonate.

Ce loft où l'ancienne structure côtoie une approche architecturale moderne, a été conçu comme un espace où la lumière naturelle est omniprésente. Ce projet couvre la restauration totale d'un espace pratiquement vide et comporte deux idées directrices : d'une part, préserver les façades et les toitures et d'autre part, construire un nouvel espace au centre de l'habitation, ancienne maison de cocher. L'architecte a su tirer parti de la structure préexistante et aussi du patio à l'arrière du bâtiment, transformé en jardin, dotant toutes les chambres de lumière naturelle et d'une sensation d'espace. En outre, grâce au maintien du design de la façade d'origine, le bâti- ment se fond avec les autres édifices environ- nants. La réception mène au salon, un espace généreux inondé de lumière qui s'ouvre sur le patio où une rangée de bambous et de paravents en poly carbonate translucide filtrent la lumière.

Dieses Loft, in dem die alte Struktur mit moder- nen Elemente kombiniert wurde, wurde als ein Raum geplant, in dem es überall Tageslicht gibt. Diese Planung, bei der ein radikaler Eingriff in einen praktisch leeren Raum vorgenommen wurde, ging von zwei Voraussetzungen aus. Einer- seits mussten die Fassaden und das Dach erhal- ten bleiben, andererseits wurde ein Neubau im Zentrum des Hauses, wo sich einst der Wagen- schuppen befand, durchgeführt. Der Architekt nutzte nicht nur die bereits vorhandene Struktur, sondern auch den Hinterhof, der heute ein Garten ist, um Licht in alle Räume zu bringen und ein Gefühl von Weite zu schaffen. Da die Originalfas- sade erhalten blieb, fügt sich das Gebäude har- monisch in die Umgebung ein. Der Korridor führt zum Wohnzimmer, ein großer, lichtdurchströmter Raum zum Hof. Eine Bambusreihe im Innenhof und Schirme aus lichtdurchlässigem Polycarbo- nat filtern das Licht vom Hof.

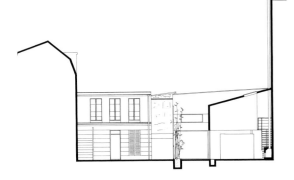

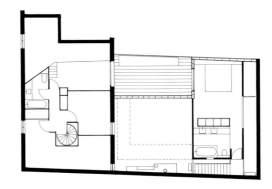

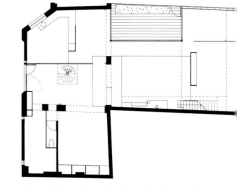

› Section Section Schnitt

› First floor Premier étage Erstes Obergeschoss

› Ground floor Rez-de-chaussée Erdgeschoss

Potter Loft

New York, United States

The refurbishment of this loft in New York's Chelsea district reflects the client's simple lifestyle. The layout is governed by the concept of open space, moving from the centrally located kitchen to the bathrooms and bedrooms at the back of the apartment. The kitchen area is surrounded by different types of surfaces that define the thresholds of the space. Concrete panels mark off the living room. Banks of lights on the dining room ceiling, including a distinctive overhead wedge-shape lamp, provide intense illumination. The building's security entrance consists of a sliding door built with a custom-made metal sheet. A pivoting door provides the bedroom with more intimacy and allows light to enter as it is opened more fully. The windows to the street provide views of the exterior, although privacy is protected by Venetian blinds, which also control the flow of light.

La rénovation de ce loft situé dans le quartier de Chelsea à New-York reflète la simplicité du style de vie du client. La conception s'articule autour d'un espace ouvert qui part de la cuisine située au centre vers les salles de bains et les chambres à coucher, à l'arrière de l'appartement. L'aire de la cuisine est entourée de différents types de revêtements qui définissent le seuil des autres espaces. Des panneaux de béton délimitent le salon. Des sources de lumière au plafond du salon, y compris une lampe spéciale angulaire, suspendue, dispensent un éclairage intense. L'entrée surveillée de l'édifice est doté d'une porte coulissante en feuille de métal construite sur commande. Une porte tournante confère plus d'intimité à la chambre et de par son ouverture, permet à la lumière d'entrer. Les fenêtres sur la rue ont vue sur l'extérieur et sont dotées de stores à l'italienne pour préserver l'intimité et contrôler le flux de lumière.

Die Sanierung dieses Loftes in Distrikt Chelsea in New York spiegelt den einfachen Lebensstil des Kunden wieder. Wichtig ist das Konzept des offenen Raumes, das die Küche im Zentrum, die Badezimmer und die Schlafzimmer hinten in der Wohnung umfasst. Der Küchenbereich ist von unterschiedlichen Oberflächen umgeben, die die Schwellen des Raums definieren. Betonplatten markieren den Wohnbereich. Lichtbalken in der Esszimmerdecke und eine seltsame, keilförmige Lampe sorgen für intensive Beleuchtung. Der Sicherheitseingang des Gebäudes besteht aus einer Schiebetür aus maßgefertigten Metallplatten. Eine schwenkbare Tür trennt das Schlafzimmer ab und lässt viel Licht herein, da sie ganz geöffnet werden kann. Durch das Fenster zur Straße hat man einen guten Ausblick, der Blick nach innen wird jedoch durch Jalousien begrenzt, die auch das Licht regulieren.

The kitchen and dining area share a common, open space, facilitating the conversation between those who are cooking and their guests.

La cuisine et la salle à manger se partagent l'espace ouvert, facilitant la conversation entre le cuisinier et ses invités.

Die Küche und der Essbereich liegen in einem gemeinsamen, sehr offenen Raum, so dass die Gastgeber sich mit ihren Gästen beim Kochen unterhalten können.

› Plan Plan Grundriss

The architect's aim was to keep the structure intact by introducing new floors to hold up the rooms without removing any of the existing brick walls.

L'architecte voulait garder la structure d'origine intacte en intégrant de nouveaux sols pour rénover les pièces sans ôter aucun des murs de briques existants.

Ziel des Architekten war es, die Struktur intakt zu erhalten, indem er neue Böden einzog, die die Räume stützen, ohne dabei die existierende Ziegelwände entfernen zu müssen.

Refurbishment of an Attic
Rénovation d'un attique
Dachgeschosssanierung

Milan, Italy

In this project, located in the historical center of Milan, the architect disregarded the space's former layout and focused on a new distribution plan. The general concept was to integrate all the rooms into a single space, avoiding doors and interior partitions. The choice of only one type of flooring–dark wood–contributes to a feeling of unity while contrasting with the clean, white walls. The architect used the sloping ceilings to create a main axis of circulation in the center of the dwelling at the highest point. The spaces for activities related to leisure and relaxation were constructed on the perimeter. The service areas–the bathroom, the kitchen, and the toilets–are monolithic volumes. Since this loft is a succession of spaces with no defined frontiers, the entryway becomes the living room, and the bedroom melts into the bathroom.

Dans ce projet, situé dans le centre historique de Milan, l'architecte n'a pas tenu compte de l'ancienne planification et s'est concentré sur un nouveau schéma. L'idée générale est d'intégrer toutes les pièces en un espace unique, éliminant portes et cloisons intérieures. Le choix d'un seul type de sol – en bois sombre – accentue la sensation d'unité et contraste avec la pureté des murs blancs. L'architecte a tiré parti des plafonds inclinés pour créer un grand axe de passage au cœur de l'habitation, en son point culminant. Les espaces consacrés au loisir et à la détente sont construits sur le pourtour. Les aires de services – salle de bains, cuisine et toilettes – sont des volumes monolithiques. Ce loft étant une succession d'espaces sans délimitations définies, l'entrée se métamorphose en salon et la chambre à coucher fusionne avec la salle de bains.

Bei diesem Projekt im historischen Stadtkern von Mailand veränderte der Architekt die ursprüngliche Raumaufteilung vollständig. Das Allgemeinkonzept war es, alle Funktionen in einem einzigen Raum unterzubringen und Türen und innere Raumteiler zu vermeiden. Der durchgehende Fußbodenbelag aus einem einzigen Material, aus dunklem Holz, trägt zu diesem Gefühl von Einheit bei und steht im Gegensatz zu den saubereren weißen Wänden. Der Architekt benutzte die geneigten Decken, um eine Hauptachse für den Durchgang in der Mitte der Wohnung, unter dem höchsten Punkt der Decke zu schaffen. Die Raumabschnitte für Freizeit und Entspannung liegen am Rand. Die funktionellen Räume wie Badezimmer, Küche und Toiletten sind monolithische Volumen. Da dieses Loft aus einer Abfolge von Räumen ohne definierte Grenzen besteht, wird aus dem Eingangsbereich das Wohnzimmer und das Schlafzimmer verschmilzt mit dem Badezimmer.

The shower, made of glass, is located in the bedroom and appears as an independent volume that is visually connected to the rest of the room.

La douche en verre forme dans la chambre à coucher un bloc indépendant relié visuellement au reste de la pièce.

Die gläserne Duschkabine befindet sich im Schlafzimmer und wirkt wie ein unabhängiges Volumen, das visuell mit dem Rest des Raumes in Verbindung steht.

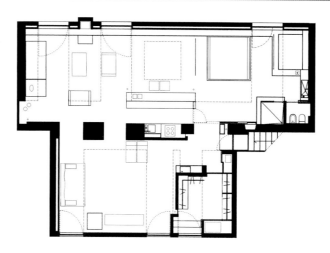

› Plan Plan Grundriss

Two lofts on Passage Gauthier
Deux lofts du Passage Gauthier
Zwei Lofts in der Passage Gauthier

Paris, France

The architects Frédéric Jung and Claudine Dreyfus refurbished this industrial building to make room for two self-contained residences that are only connected by a communal terrace on the upper floor. Both units had to be independent of each other, so the architects divided the building with a vertical wall and added another level. The conversion focused its attention more on the construction and design than the details, reflecting the building's location and the precision of the architectural project. The interior program developed an extremely dynamic vertical concept, in a sequence centered on the helicoidal staircases in each loft. The same principle was applied in both spaces, involving a large living room and several blocks that make up the bedrooms, the bathrooms and the closets. The terrace, with a floor of wooden planks, gazes out over the streets of Paris.

Les architectes Frédéric Jung et Claudine Dreyfus ont restauré ce bâtiment industriel pour y installer deux résidences mitoyennes qui partagent une terrasse commune à l'étage supérieur, trait d'union entre les deux. Les deux unités devant être indépendantes l'une de l'autre, les architectes ont divisé le bâtiment par un mur vertical et ont rajouté un deuxième niveau. Ce projet de restauration, davantage axé sur la construction et le design que sur les détails, reflète la situation du bâtiment et la précision de la conception architecturale. Le concept intérieur développe une dynamique verticale extrême autour de l'axe représenté par l'escalier hélicoïdal de chaque loft. Les deux habitations sont régies par le même principe de base, à savoir un grand salon et une série de blocs pour les chambres, les salles de bains et les toilettes. De la terrasse, en lattes de bois, la vue s'étend sur les rues de Paris.

Die Architekten Frédéric Jung und Claudine Dreyfus sanierten dieses Industriegebäude, um zwei unabhängige Wohnungen zu schaffen, die durch eine Terrasse im Obergeschoss verbunden sind. Beide Einheiten sollten selbständig sein, deshalb unterteilten die Architekten das Gebäude mit einer vertikalen Wand und fügten eine weitere Ebene hinzu. Bei der Gestaltung der Wohnungen wurde das Augenmerk mehr auf die Konstruktion und das Design als auf die Einzelheiten gerichtet. Dadurch wird der Standort des Gebäudes und die Präzision der architektonischen Planung reflektiert. Die Raumgestaltung basiert auf einem dynamischen, vertikalen Konzept, eine Sequenz, die auf der spiralförmigen Treppe in jedem Loft beruht. In beiden Einheiten folgt die Raumgestaltung auf dem gleichen Prinzip, ein großes Wohnzimmer und verschiedene Blöcke Badezimmer und Wandschränke formen. Die Terrasse mit dem Boden aus Holzbrettern ragt über die Straßen von Paris.

Although the street façade remains practically unchanged, two panels of glass bricks have been put into the rear to allow sunlight to penetrate inside.

La façade reste pratiquement inchangée à l'exception de deux cloisons de pavés de verre installées à l'arrière du bâtiment pour permettre à la lumière de pénétrer l'intérieur.

Die Fassade zur Straße hin blieb fast unverändert, während man an der Hinterfassade zwei Platten aus Glasbausteinen eingesetzt hat, damit Tageslicht in die Räume fallen kann.

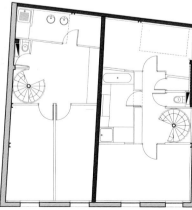

› Ground floor Rez-de-chaussée Erdgeschoss

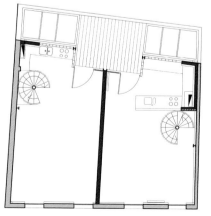

› First floor Premier étage Erstes Obergeschoss

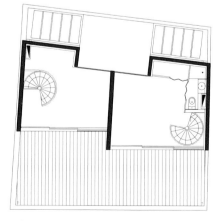

› Second floor Deuxième étage Zweite Obergeschoss

The interior program developed an extremely dynamic vertical concept, involving a large, open living room.

L'intérieur, conçu selon un concept de verticalité général, possède un salon large et ouvert.

Die Innengestaltung erfolgte nach einem sehr dynamischen, vertikalen Konzept, zu dem ein großes, offenes Wohnzimmer gehörte.

New York, United States

Baron Loft

The architect Deborah Berke focused on the perfecting and reducing the elements to achieve a pure and elegant minimalist style in this renovation for an art director and his family. The materials used include smooth plaster on the walls, while the flooring is of ebonized oak. Polished schist blocks where used in the bathroom, next to oiled walnut slabs, brushed stainless steel splashes, white glass, and white window scrims. Each of these materials has the least details possible. Much of the furniture is built into the house and displays the owner's extensive art collection. A strict color palette gives way to a sober design sprinkled with subtle doses of warm tones. The kitchen is hidden behind walnut doors, while a translucent glass wall conceals the master bedroom.

Dans ce projet de rénovation pour un directeur artistique et sa famille, l'architecte Deborah Berke a misé sur la perfection et la réduction des éléments pour obtenir un style minimaliste épuré tout en élégance. Les matériaux se déclinent en plâtres lisses pour les murs. Les sols sont en chêne aux allures d'ébène. Des dalles d'ardoise polie ont été posées dans la salle de bains, en alternance avec des lattes de noyer huilé, des touches d'acier inoxydable brossé, du verre blanc comme les châssis de fenêtre. Chacun de ces matériaux est dépourvu de motifs. L'importante collection d'œuvre d'art du propriétaire est exposée sur les meubles intégrés à l'architecture de la maison. Un nuancier de couleurs sobres met en valeur un design aux lignes épurées, ponctuées des touches subtiles de teintes chaudes. La cuisine se cache derrière des murs en noyer et une paroi de verre translucide dissimule la chambre des maîtres.

Die Architektin Deborah Berke konzentrierte sich auf eine Perfektion und Reduktion von Elementen, um einen reinen, eleganten und minimalistischen Stil bei dieser Renovierung für einen Art Director und seine Familie zu erzielen. Die Wände sind weich verputzt, die Fußböden mit gebeizter Eiche belegt. Die im Badezimmer verwendeten Materialien sind polierte Schieferblöcke, Tafeln aus geöltem Nussbaum, Vorrichtungen zum Schutz vor Wasser aus gebürstetem Edelstahl, Milchglas und weiße Leinengardinen. All diese Materialien sind so einfach wie möglich. Viele Möbel sind eingebaut und dienen als Ausstellungselemente für die umfassende Kunstsammlung des Eigentümers. Eine strenge Farbpalette lässt die Gestaltung sehr schlicht wirken, vereinzelt werden gezielt warme Töne eingesetzt. Die Küche liegt hinter Türen aus Nussbaum verborgen, das Hauptschlafzimmer liegt hinter einer lichtdurchlässigen Glaswand.

The lighting, red furniture, and ebonized oak floors add color and so set up a contrast with the plain white walls.

L'éclairage, le mobilier rouge et les sols en chêne couleur ébène ajoutent une note de couleur qui contraste avec la blancheur des murs.

Die leuchtend roten Möbel und die schwarz gebeizte Eichenböden setzen Farbakzente und dienen als Kontrast zu den schlichten, weißen Wänden.

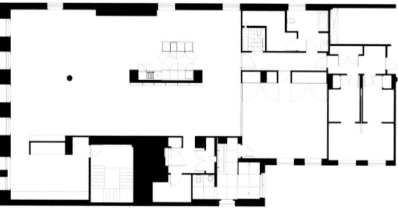

› Plan Plan Grundriss

Some of the furniture is built into the house and display the owner's extensive art collection.

Une partie du mobilier est intégrée à la maison et permet d'exposer l'importante collection du maître des lieux.

Einige der Möbel sind eingebaut und dienen als Ausstellungselemente für die umfassende Kunstsammlung des Eigentümers.

Loft Paris 10ème

Paris, France

A façade of glass bricks–a vestige of the paint and wallpaper store that once occupied the premises–conceals a large space on the ground floor and basement that was converted into a warm, light-filled loft residence. In order for the light to penetrate everywhere the conversion removed part of the ceilings that separated the floors in the entrance and in the rear. Glass bricks were also used in the inner walls, blurring the view so that light can reach the bedrooms without any loss of privacy. The ground floor was designed to achieve a warm, homely atmosphere for the bedrooms and the office, while the basement is a large space containing the communal areas. The axis of the home is a glass and stainless steel staircase that adds to the interplay of light; it goes right into the kitchen, where it even serves as a table.

La façade de briques de verre – vestige du magasin de papiers peints situé sur ce site – abrite un rez-de-chaussée et un sous-sol, immense espace converti en un loft chaleureux et inondé de lumière naturelle. Une partie des plafonds séparant les espaces a été supprimée à l'entrée et à l'arrière, pour laisser pénétrer un maximum de lumière. Les murs intérieurs, également en briques de verre translucides, mais non transparentes, permettent à la lumière de pénétrer dans les chambres tout en préservant l'intimité. Le design du rez-de-chaussée crée une atmosphère douillette et chaude dans les chambres et le bureau. Quant au sous-sol, il est très spacieux et abrite les parties communes. L'escalier de verre et d'acier inoxydable est l'axe de l'appartement dont il accentue le jeu de lumière. Il s'inscrit cœur de la cuisine où il se métamorphose en table.

Eine Fassade aus Glasziegeln, die noch aus dem ehemaligen Farb- und Tapetengeschäft stammt, das sich einst hier befand, verbirgt große Räume im Erd- und Kellergeschoss, die zu einer warmen und hellen Wohnung umgebaut wurden. Damit das Tageslicht überall hin gelangen konnte, wurden Teile der Decke entfernt, die die Stockwerke am Eingang und im hinteren Teil trennten. Ebenso wurden Glasbausteine für die Innenwände verwendet, die Licht durchlassen, aber die Privatsphäre schützen. Die Atmosphäre im Erdgeschoss, wo sich die Schlafzimmer und das Büro befinden, ist sehr freundlich, das Kellergeschoss hingegen ist ein weiter, offener, von allen genutzter Raum. Die Achse dieser Wohnung ist die Treppe aus Glas und Edelstahl, die das Spiel mit dem Licht noch unterstreicht. Sie führt bis in die Küche, wo sie sogar als Tisch dient.

The home revolves around a glass and stainless-steel staircase that adds to the interplay of light characteristic of the entire space.

La maison évolue autour d'un escalier d'acier et de verre qui accentue le jeu de lumière, point d'orgue de l'espace entier.

Das Loft ist um eine Treppe aus Glas und Edelstahl angelegt, was das Spiel mit dem Licht, das den Raum prägt, noch unterstreicht.

› Ground floor Rez-de-chaussée Erdgeschoss

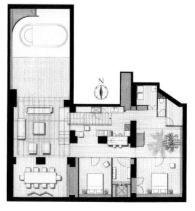

› Basement Sous-sol Kellergeschoss

The ground floor was designed to achieve a warm, cozy atmosphere for the bedrooms and the office, while the basement is a large, open space.

Le rez-de-chaussée est conçu pour créer une atmosphère chaleureuse et agréable dans les chambres et le bureau alors que le sous-sol est un espace généreux et ouvert.

Die Atmosphäre im Erdgeschoss, wo sich die Schlafzimmer und das Büro befinden, ist sehr warm und einladend, das Kellergeschoss hingegen ist ein weiter, offener Raum.

Orange and White
Orange et blanc
Orange und Weiß

Buenos Aires, Argentina

Based on simple lines combined with the use of noble materials, this project features a dynamic space in which each area possesses it own characteristic. Dark woods, natural stone, steel, and translucent fabrics in different textures are the most prominent materials, while neutral colors with different intensities create a soothing environment. The kitchen is concealed within a module alongside the entrance hall and incorporates a breakfast area with stools. The lounge, comfortably furnished and decorated in bright orange and white, leads to the upper level, which contains the bedroom suite. The views between the various spaces are filtered by dividing elements, such as the large, sliding wooden door that constitutes one of the home's main decorative features and disappears into the wall to reveal the bedroom. An en-suite bathroom reveals an open washing area and a more private shower and toilet.

Ce projet, qui allie lignes épurées et matériaux nobles, met en scène un espace dynamique où chaque zone a ses propres caractéristiques. Bois foncés, pierre naturelle, acier et voiles transparents de textures différentes sont les principaux matériaux qui régissent cette atmosphère calme, créée par un dégradé de couleurs claires plus ou moins intenses. Le long de l'entrée, un module abrite la cuisine et un coin repas doté de tabourets. Le séjour, aux meubles confortables et au décor dans les tons d'orange et de blanc soutenus, mène à l'étage supérieur où se trouve la grande chambre à coucher. Des éléments de partition tamisent la vue entre les divers espaces, à l'image de grandes portes coulissantes de bois avant de disparaître dans le mur pour nous révéler la chambre à coucher. Une salle de bains, à l'instar d'une suite, s'ouvre sur une salle d'eau puis sur une sphère plus intime avec douche et toilettes.

Die Gestalter schufen einfache Linien in Kombination mit edlen Materialien. So entstanden dynamische Räume, in denen jeder Bereich seinen eigenen Charakter hat. Dunkles Holz, Naturstein, Stahl und lichtdurchlässige Gewebe in verschiedenen Texturen sind die hauptsächlich verwendeten Materialien. Neutrale Farben in verschiedener Stärke schaffen eine sanfte Umgebung. Die Küche ist hinter einem Modul verborgen, das am Eingangskorridor entlang verläuft und den Frühstücksbereich mit Stühlen enthält. Das in hellorange und weiß dekorierte Wohnzimmer führt auf die obere Ebene, wo sich das große Schlafzimmer befindet. Die Blicke zwischen den verschiedenen Bereichen werden durch Trennelemente aufgefangen. Eins davon ist die Schiebetür aus Holz die ganz in der Wand verschwinden kann, um das Schlafzimmer offen zu lassen. Dort gibt es ein Badezimmer mit einem offenen Waschbereich und einer geschlossenen Zone für Dusche und Toilette.

Comprised of comfortable furniture and bright shades of white and orange, the living area leads to the upper level, which contains the bedroom suite.

Doté de meubles confortables et de tons soutenus blancs et oranges, le salon mène à l'étage supérieur où se trouve la chambre à coucher, à l'instar d'une suite.

Der Wohnbereich ist mit bequemen Möbeln und in hellen Weiß- und Orangetönen dekoriert und führt in die obere Ebene, in der sich das große Schlafzimmer befindet.

The interaction between the proportions of the horizontal spaces and the vertical voids, as well as the amount of natural light, serve to mark out the various areas in the loft.

L'interaction entre les espaces horizontaux et les vides verticaux, ainsi que le volume de la lumière naturelle, permettent de délimiter les espaces du loft.

Durch die Wechselwirkung zwischen des Proportionen der horizontalen Räume und der vertikalen Hohlräume, sowie durch das einströmende Tageslicht werden die verschieden Bereiche in diesem Loft markiert.

The kitchen is concealed within a module alongside the entrance hallway and incorporates a breakfast area with stools.

Le long du hall d'entrée, un module abrite la cuisine et un coin repas doté de tabourets.

Die Küche ist hinter einem Modul verborgen, das am Eingangskorridor entlang verläuft. Hier gibt es eine Frühstücksecke mit Stühlen

White walls and neutral colors of different intensities create a soothing setting environment in which special elements stand out.

Murs blancs et couleurs neutres, d'intensités différentes créent un environnement apaisant où certains éléments sont mis en valeur.

Weiße Wände und neutrale Farben verschiedener Stärke schaffen eine sanfte Wohnatmosphäre, in der einzelne Elemente auffallen.

the bedroom, a window behind the bed looks onto the lower level, and an en-suite bathroom reveals an open wash area and a more private shower and toilet.

ans la chambre à coucher, une fenêtre derrière le lit permet de voir le niveau inférieur et une salle de bains, en forme de suite, révèle une salle d'eau ouverte et une sphère plus int-
e avec douche et toilettes.

Schlafzimmer sieht man von einem Fenster hinter dem Bett aus bis zur unteren Ebene. Das Badezimmer, das im gleichen Raum untergebracht ist, hat einen offenen Waschbe-
ich und eine privatere Zone für die Dusche und Toilette.

Loft in London
Loft à Londres
Loft in London

London, United Kingdom

The firm Child Graddon Lewis converted this charming Victorian building in the heart of Covent Garden into loft-style apartments. They created 22 shells in the building, originally designed as a warehouse. The apartments are distributed over six stories, with a retail space on the ground floor. Flexibility lies at the heart of the design concept, which gives clients the freedom to create their own interior layout and develop their own truly unique space. The company designed the kitchen, the bathroom and some pieces of furniture, which were put at the disposal of the new owners. Carefully chosen additions like large sliding doors lead to balconies and terraces constructed with cedar flooring. New metal-framed windows and glass panels take advantage of the natural light entering the apartments. Outside, the designers adapted the historic building to create a stunning rear elevation that capitalizes on period details.

L'entreprise Child Graddon Lewis a converti ce charmant édifice victorien, au cœur de Covent Garden, dans des logements style loft. Ils ont créé 22 modules, destinés à l'origine pour un entrepôt. Les appartements sont répartis sur six étages, le rez-de-chaussée étant réservé à un espace commercial. La flexibilité s'inscrit au cœur du concept design, permettant ainsi au client de moduler l'espace intérieur à sa guise pour créer un univers personnel et unique. La compagnie a conçu la cuisine, la salle de bains et certains meubles, mis à la disposition des nouveaux propriétaires ainsi que des éléments supplémentaires, bien choisis : portes coulissantes sur balcons et terrasses construites en bois de cèdre. Fenêtres à châssis de métal et cloisons de verre favorisent l'entrée de la lumière naturelle dans les appartements. A l'extérieur, les designers ont rehaussé à merveille la façade de l'édifice historique mettant en relief les détails d'époque.

Das Unternehmen Child Graddon Lewis baute dieses viktorianische Gebäude in Covent Garden in eine Reihe von Lofts um. Sie schufen 22 Einheiten in dem Gebäude, das einst als Lagerhaus diente. Die Appartements liegen auf 6 Stockwerken, im Erdgeschoss befindet sich ein Geschäft. Grundlage des Konzeptes war die Vielseitigkeit, so dass die Kunden die Möglichkeit hatten, die Räume selbst zu gestalten und einzigartig zu machen. Das Unternehmen entwarf die Küche, das Badezimmer und ein paar Möbelstücke, die den neuen Besitzern zur Verfügung gestellt wurden. Zusätzliche Elemente wurden sorgfältig ausgewählt, wie z. B. die Schiebetüren zu den Balkonen und Terrassen mit Böden aus Zedernholz. Neue Fenster mit Metallrahmen und Glasplatten lassen das Tageslicht in die Appartements dringen. Auch von außen veränderten die Architekten das historische Gebäude, indem sie eine verblüffende Erhebung bauten, um die historischen Elemente zu betonen.

The sink and floors are made of wood and the walls are clad with stone. The kitchen is a very practical and comfortable part of the house.

L'évier et les sols sont en bois et les murs sont habillés de pierre. La cuisine est un endroit de la maison où pratique et confort vont de paire.

Der Spülstein und die Fußböden bestehen aus Holz und die Wände sind mit Stein verkleidet. Die Küche ist sehr praktisch und komfortabel.

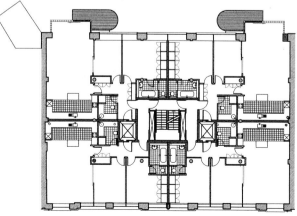

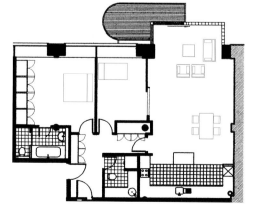

› Plans Plans Grundrisse

London, United Kingdom

Nile Street Loft

This apartment is located on the top floor and roof level of a nineteenth-century-warehouse in London. The façades were left untreated and the existing brickwork and floor slabs were exposed, while new service areas were located near the front door. The client's brief called for a one-bedroom apartment with home office space and a multi-purpose room that can be closed off and used as a second bedroom. The layout maximizes the sense of space by moving the original front door and creating a double-height entrance hall that visually connects the two floor levels and contains all the circulation areas. A skylight runs the full length of the top floor over this area, spreading natural light deep inside. The several large sliding and pivoting fire doors are hidden from view, ensuring a fluid relationship with the open-plan living/dining/kitchen areas while fulfilling their function in the case of a fire.

Cet appartement est situé au dernier étage, au niveau du toit d'un entrepôt londonien du XIXe siècle. Les façades ont été laissées à l'état initial, la maçonnerie et les planchers mis en valeur. De nouvelles zones de services ont été installées près de la porte d'entrée. Le cahier des charges exigeait un appartement d'une chambre avec un bureau et une pièce polyvalente utilisable comme deuxième chambre, une fois fermée. Le concept optimalise la sensation d'espace en déplaçant la porte d'entrée d'origine et créant une entrée à double hauteur, lien visuel entre les deux étages, permettant l'accès à toutes les pièces. Un velux s'étend sur toute la longueur du dernier étage, inondant l'intérieur de lumière naturelle. Les grandes portes coulissantes et pivotantes ignifugées sont escamotables, conférant une grande fluidité entre les espaces ouverts salon/ salle à manger/cuisine, tout en remplissant leur rôle en cas d'incendie.

Das Apartment befindet sich im Ober- und Dachgeschoss eines ehemaligen Londoner Warenhauses aus dem 19. Jh.. Die Fassaden blieben unverändert und die existierenden Ziegelmauern und Bodenfliesen wurden zu einem sichtbaren Element, während neue Servicebereiche bei der Eingangstür geschaffen wurden. Der Kunde wünschte sich ein Schlafzimmer, ein Heimbüro und einen Mehrzweckraum, den man abtrennen und als zweites Schlafzimmer benutzen kann. Die Vordertür wurde verschoben und ein Korridor doppelter Höhe geschafen, der die beiden Etagen visuell miteinander verbindet, alle Durchgangsbereiche umfasst und den Raum größer wirken lässt. Über dem Obergeschoss befindet sich ein Dachfenster, durch das Licht in die ganze Wohnung dringt. Die verschiedenen gleitenden oder schwenkbaren Feuertüren wurden verborgen, so dass eine fließende Beziehung zwischen den offenen bereichen entstand.

The most important of the new elements is the African walnut wall panel, which extends from the open kitchen to the entrance hall and establishes a cohesive, predominantly natural feel

La cloison en noyer d'Afrique, qui s'étend de la cuisine ouverte au hall d'entrée, est le plus important des nouveaux éléments, conférant à l'ensemble une impression d'unité avec une prédominance de la nature.

Das wichtigste, neue Element ist die Wandtafel aus Afrikanischem Nussbaum, das von der offenen Küche bis zum Eingangsbereich reicht. So entsteht eine zusammenhängende, sehr natürliche Atmosphäre.

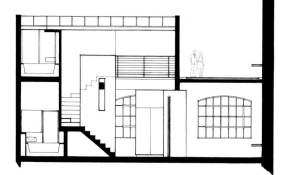

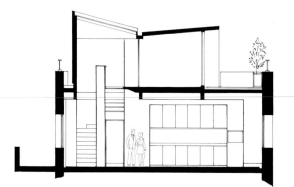

› Sections Sections Schnitte

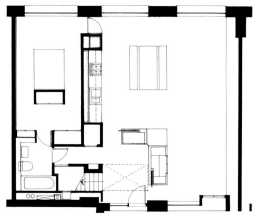

› Ground floor Rez-de-chaussée Erdgeschoss

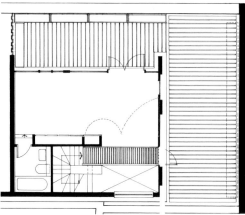

› First floor Premier étage Erstes Obergeschoss

154

The bedroom is in one of the corners on the upper level. The terrace was covered with wooden sheets and has magnificent views of the city skyline.

La chambre se trouve dans l'un des angles de l'étage supérieur. La terrasse est revêtue de lattes de bois et offre une vue magnifique sur la ligne d'horizon de la ville.

Das Schlafzimmer liegt in einer der Ecken der oberen Etage. Die überdachte Terrasse ist mit Holzplatten gedeckt, man hat einen wundervollen Blick auf die Skyline der Stadt.

156

skylight runs the full length of the top floor, spreading natural light deep into the home.

n velux court le long du toit, inondant toute la maison de lumière.

ber dem gesamten Obergeschoss befindet sich ein Dachfenster, durch das Licht in die ganze Wohnung dringt.

Brown Loft

An open plan, an emphasis on perspective and muted palette of materials characterize this Soho loft. Part of a renovated industrial building, the space was fitted out for an artist and illustrator who wanted a space for living, working, and entertaining clients. The building's original columns were retained and restored, acting as a polished foil for the modernity of the renovation. Their presence creates an invisible line between the kitchen and living areas. Translucent acrylic and aluminum partitions allow for flexible divisions between the major spaces and disappear discreetly into pockets in the wall. A kitchen island was inserted into the open-plan space, acting simultaneously as a working surface, eating table, and divider between kitchen and living areas. Industrial attributes, such as the sprinkler pipes along the ceiling, were restored and kept exposed as a reminder of the building's original state.

Un plan ouvert, l'accent mis sur la perspective et un petit éventail de matériaux caractérisent ce loft de Soho. Partie d'un bâtiment industriel restauré, l'espace a été agencé pour un artiste illustrateur pour y vivre, y travailler et recevoir des clients. Les colonnes originales du bâtiment ont été gardées et restaurées, redonnant tout son lustre à la modernité de la rénovation. Leur présence crée une ligne invisible entre la cuisine et les pièces à vivre. Cloisons en aluminium et acrylique translucide permettent de moduler les espaces principaux. Elles disparaissent discrètement dans des fentes murales. Un îlot central a été installé dans l'espace ouvert de la cuisine, faisant office à la fois de plan de travail, de table et de partition entre la cuisine et les pièces à vivre. Les éléments d'usine, à l'instar des tuyaux d'arrosage au plafond, ont été restaurés et conservés en souvenir de l'édifice d'antan.

Offenheit, betonte Perspektiven und eine beschränkte Materialpalette charakterisieren dieses Loft in Soho. In einem renovierten Fabrikgebäude sollten Wohn- und Arbeitsräume und ein Gäste- und Kundenbereich für die Auftraggeber (Künstler und Illustrator) geschaffen werden. Die vorhandenen Säulen wurden restauriert; sie dienen als eine Art aufpolierter Hintergrund für die Modernität der Renovierung und ziehen eine unsichtbare Linie zwischen der Küche und den Wohnbereichen. Diese Raumteilungen aus lichtdurchlässiges Acryl und Aluminium dienen als veränderliche Abgrenzungen zwischen den Hauptbereichen. In den offenen Raum wurde eine Kücheninsel eingesetzt, die als Arbeitsfläche und Esstisch dient. Industrielle Elemente wie die Sprinklerrohre an der Decke wurden restauriert und blieben sichtbar, um an die Ursprünge des Gebäudes zu erinnern.

Translucent acrylic and aluminum partitions allow for flexible divisions between the main spaces but can disappear discreetly into pockets in the wall.

Des cloisons en acrylique translucide ou en aluminium permettent de moduler à souhait les espaces principaux et disparaissent rapidement dans des fentes murales.

Raumteiler aus lichtdurchlässigem Akryl und Aluminium dienen als veränderliche Abgrenzungen zwischen den Hauptbereichen, sie können aber auch diskret in dafür vorgesehene Wandöffnungen verborgen werden.

› Plan Plan Grundriss

Loft on Avenue Philippe Auguste
Loft de l'avenue Philippe Auguste
Loft in der Avenue Philippe Auguste

Paris, France

Situated in a quiet, sunny patio, this loft, originally part of a mirror store dating from 1920, was refurbished as a home and work space for a young couple without children. The redbrick building topped with a glass and metal structure, hampered by its limited size and lack of sunlight on part of the ground floor, required an intervention that concentrated on making the most of these restricted possibilities. Thus, the architects divided the space into a work studio, next to with the garden terrace on the ground floor, while the other rooms are on the first floor. The need to achieve the greatest possible spaciousness demanded the removal of barriers and opaque surfaces: the façade was made of glass, to capture the maximum amount of sunlight and extend the visual space of the interior into the patio dotted with trees. Moreover, the different areas are marked off by variations in the floor height, and by panels made of translucent or transparent materials.

Situé dans un patio calme et ensoleillé, ce loft faisait partie, à l'origine, d'une miroiterie de 1920. Il a été restauré en espace habitable et en bureau pour un couple sans enfants. Le bâtiment de briques rouges, coiffé d'une structure en verre et métal, souffrait de sa petite taille et du manque de lumière naturelle sur une partie du rez-de-chaussée. Le but de la restauration était de maximaliser cet espace malgré de faibles possibilités. Les architectes ont donc divisé l'espace en un studio faisant office de bureau, à côté du jardin terrasse au rez-de-chaussée. Les autres pièces se trouvent au premier étage. Le besoin impératif d'espace a nécessité le retrait de cloisons et de surfaces opaques : la nouvelle façade de verre permet de capter le maximum de soleil et de prolonger l'espace visuel de l'intérieur vers le patio arboré. En outre, les différentes zones sont délimitées par les différences de hauteur du sol et par des cloisons en matériaux translucides ou transparents.

Dieses Loft in einem ruhigen, sonnigen Hof war einst Teil eines Spiegelgeschäftes aus dem Jahr 1920. Es wurde zu einer Wohnung und einem Arbeitsraum für ein kinderloses Paar umgebaut. Das Gebäude aus rotem Ziegelstein ist relativ klein und ein Teil des Erdgeschosses war sehr dunkel. Dies stellte eine Herausforderung für die Planer dar. Deshalb unterteilten die Architekten den Raum in ein Studio in der Nähe der Gartenterrasse im Erdgeschoss, während die anderen Räume in der ersten Etage liegen. Da soviel Raum wie möglich gewonnen werden musste, wurden viele Barrieren und lichtundurchlässige Oberflächen entfernt. Die Fassade ist aus Glas, um soviel Sonnenlicht wie möglich einzufangen und auch visuell den Raum in den baumbestandenen Innenhof auszudehnen. Die verschiedenen Bereiche werden durch unterschiedliche Fußbodenhöhen und Paneele aus lichtdurchlässigem oder transparentem Material voneinander abgegrenzt.

The different areas are marked off by both variations in the floor height and panels made of translucent or transparent materials.

Les différentes zones sont définies à la fois par les variations de hauteur des sols et par les cloisons translucides ou transparentes.

Die verschiedenen Zonen werden durch unterschiedliche Fußbodenhöhen und Paneele aus lichtdurchlässigem oder transparentem Material voneinander abgegrenzt.

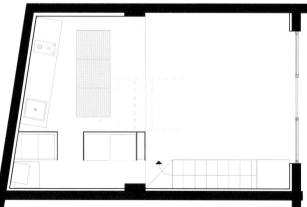

› Ground floor Rez-de-chaussée Erdgeschoss

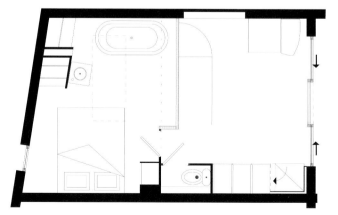

› First floor Premier étage Erstes Obergeschoss

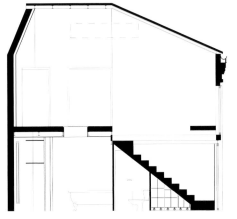
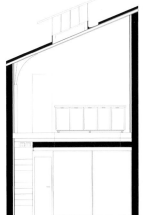

Marnix Warehouse
Entrepôt Marnix
Marnix Lagerhaus

Antwerp, Belgium

Guided by the context of the project and the identity of their clients, these Belgian architects transformed a late-nineteenth-century warehouse into a dynamic living space. Situated on the north edge of the city, next to a large harbor, this brick building had three major compartments constructed with oak beams and pine planks. Three cubes were created: the first floats above the ground floor and contains two bathrooms. The second, situated halfway up the loft, contains a bedroom and the kitchen. The third cube hangs from the ceiling and contains a crow's-nest bedroom. The cubes are not only functional but also mark out the circulation: cantilevered oak planks emerge from one of them as a staircase leading to the roof terrace. The abstract objects relate to each other through size and form, while the white plaster and translucent glass renew the old structure of wooden beams and pillars.

Guidés par la nature du projet et la personnalité des clients, ces architectes belges ont transformé un entrepôt de la fin du XIXe siècle, en un espace de vie dynamique. Situé sur la périphérie nord de la ville, près d'un grand port, ce bâtiment en briques est divisé en trois grands espaces principaux dotés de poutres en chêne et de madriers de pin. On a conçu trois cubes: le premier flotte au-dessus du rez-de-chaussée et contient deux salles de bains. Le deuxième, au milieu du loft, abrite une chambre à coucher et une cuisine. Le troisième, suspendu au plafond tel un nid d'aigle, héberge une chambre à coucher. Outre leur rôle fonctionnel, les cubes servent à marquer le passage : des suspensions en cantilever de madriers de chêne émergent de l'un d'eux, sous forme d'escalier pour mener à la terrasse de toit. La forme et la taille font l'unisson entre les objets abstraits, le plâtre blanc et le verre translucide le lien avec l'ancienne structure de poutres et piliers de bois.

Die belgischen Architekten ließen sich von dem Kontext des Gebäudes und der Persönlichkeit ihrer Kunden inspirieren, um ein Lagerhaus aus dem 19. Jh. in einen dynamischen Wohnraum umzugestalten. Das Ziegelsteingebäude mit drei großen Gebäudeteilen aus Eichenbalken und Kieferplanken befindet sich in der Nähe eines großen Hafens. Es wurden drei Würfel geschaffen, der erste schwebt über dem Erdgeschoss und enthält die beiden Badezimmer. In dem zweiten auf halber Höhe sind ein Schlafzimmer und die Küche untergebracht. Der dritte hängt von der Decke und enthält ein Schlafzimmer im Stil eines Mastkorbes. Die Würfel sind funktionell und markieren die Wege im Wohnbereich. Aus einem der Würfel entspringen freitragende Eichenplanken, als Treppe zur Dachterrasse. Die abstrakten Objekte stehen in ihrer Größe und Form zueinander in Verbindung. Weißer Gips und durchscheinendes Glas erneuern die alte Struktur.

The cubes relate to each other through size and form, while the white plaster and translucent glass renew the old structure of wooden beams and pillars.

La taille et la forme font l'unisson entre les cubes. Le plâtre blanc et le verre translucide créent un trait d'union avec l'ancienne structure de poutres et piliers de bois.

Die Würfel stehen in ihrer Größe und Form zueinander in Verbindung. Weißer Gips und durchscheinendes Glas erneuern die alte Struktur aus Holzbalken und Pfeilern.

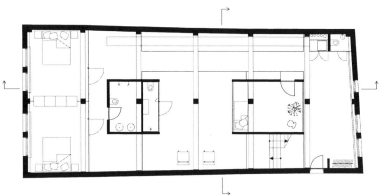

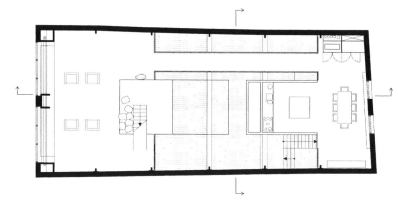

› Ground floor   Rez-de-chaussée   Erdgeschoss

› First floor   Premier étage   Erstes Obergeschoss

The living room is an open space where sunshine can flow in through the light roof coverings.

Le salon est un espace ouvert où le soleil entre à flots par la structure légère de la couverture

Das Wohnzimmer ist ein offener Raum, der von Sonnenlicht durchströmt wird, das durch de helle Dachbedeckung fällt.

Sandblasted glass is the only barrier between the shower, which is placed in one of the cubes and the adjoining living room.

Le verre poli au jet de sable est le seul écran masquant la douche placée dans l'un des cubes, à côté du salon.

Die einzige Trennwand zwischen der in einem der Würfel befindlichen Dusche und dem anliegenden Wohnzimmer ist aus sandgestrahltem Glas.

Loft in Venice
Loft à Venise
Loft in Venedig

Venice, Italy

Located close to a large Venetian church, this loft was once an important nineteenth-century foundry. The restoration project (supervised by the owner himself) sought to maintain the existing structure while transforming the space into a home that would respond to the needs of its tenants. The considerable height of the ceiling made it possible to insert a mezzanine that acts as a catwalk offering views of the church dome and the patio paved with stone. The wood and metal staircase leads down to a small studio, which is partitioned off from the surrounding living and dining areas. All the installations are concealed beneath the birch-wood floors. The furnishings are designed by the owner, except for the sixteenth-century Iberian monetiere. Solid wooden trusses, brick walls and glass doors guarantee a translucent space full of character in this post-industrial loft in Venice.

A deux pas d'une église vénitienne, ce loft est une ancienne fonderie notoire du XIXe siècle. Le projet de rénovation (conduit par le propriétaire en personne) vise à conserver la structure en place tout en la transformant en une demeure adaptée aux besoins de ses occupants. La hauteur considérable du plafond permet d'y intégrer une mezzanine, à l'instar d'une passerelle permettant de voir le toit de l'église et le patio pavé. L'escalier, conjuguant le bois et le fer, conduit à un petit studio, séparé du salon et de la salle à manger. Tous les équipements sont cachés sous les sols en bois de bouleau. Le propriétaire a dessiné les meubles, à l'exception d'une bonnetière espagnole du XVIe siècle. Poutres en bois massif, murs de briques et portes en verre confèrent transparence et originalité à ce loft post-industriel de Venise.

Dieses Loft in der Nähe einer großen, venezianischen Kirche war einst, im 19. Jh., eine bedeutende Gießerei. Bei der Renovierung, die vom Eigetümer selbst beaufsichtigt wurde, versuchte man die existierende Struktur zu erhalten und gleichzeitig den Raum in ein Zuhause zu verwandeln, das den Bedürfnissen seiner Bewohner entspricht. Aufgrund der außergewöhnlich hohen Decke konnte ein Zwischengeschoss eingefügt werden, von dem aus man einen guten Blick auf die Kirche und den mit Stein gepflasterten Innenhof hat. Die Treppe aus Holz und Metall führt in ein kleines Studio, das von den umgebenden Wohn- und Essbereichen abgetrennt ist. Alle Installationen sind unter den Birkenholzböden verborgen. Bis auf die den Iberischen Münzschrank aus dem 16. Jh. sind alle Möbel vom Eigentümer selbst entworfen. Solides Holzfachwerk, Ziegelwände und Glastüren machen dieses postindustrielle Loft in Venedig zu einem eigenwilligen, hellen Raum.

A combination of Asian style and Italian tradition characterizes this loft designed by an antique collector.

L'alliance de style asiatique et de la tradition italienne définit ce loft conçu par un collectionneur d'antiquités

Eine Kombination des asiatischen Stils mit italienischer Tradition charakterisiert dieses Loft, das von einem Antiquitätensammler gestaltet wurde.

The dining area and adjacent courtyard are examples of the Asian influence on the design, while the kitchen illustrates the Italian style.

Le design de la salle à manger et de la cour adjacente reflète l'influence asiatique, tandis que la cuisine relève du style italien.

Der Essbereich und der anliegende Hof sind Beispiele für den asiatischen Einfluss, während die Küche ganz klar im italienischen Stil gehalten ist.

The interior of the loft provides a beautiful view of the beautiful basilica nearby.

L'intérieur du loft s'ouvre sur la vue magnifique de la basilique proche.

Vom Inneren des Lofts aus hat man einen wundervollen Blick auf die benachbarte Basilika.

Loft on Rue Bichat
Loft de la rue Bichat
Loft in der Rue Bichat

Paris, France

The architect responsible for the restoration of this old two-story warehouse sought to maintain the existing structure without making any modification to its façades. This led to the idea of accentuating the contrast between the existing structure and the additions. The first step was to highlight the structure by endowing it with playful shapes and bright colors, thereby emphasizing its presence and calling attention to its use. Another determining factor of the intervention was the maximum possible exploitation of natural light. The façade was stripped of any elements that disturbed the flow of light and a large, diamond-shape window was installed to distribute the illumination. Furthermore, the empty space under the staircase was used as a means of allowing light to penetrate into the interior.

L'architecte responsable de la restauration de cet entrepôt à deux étages a essayé de maintenir la structure préexistante sans en modifier les façades. L'idée était de souligner le contraste entre cette structure existante et les parties rajoutées. Il fallait d'abord accentuer la structure en la parant de formes ludiques aux couleurs vives pour en exalter l'aspect et la fonction. Le programme de restauration s'est ensuite consacré à l'exploitation maximum de la lumière naturelle. La façade est libérée de tout élément gênant par une grande fenêtre en forme de diamant qui distribue la lumière. En outre, le vide sous l'escalier est utilisé pour laisser pénétrer la lumière à l'intérieur.

Der Architekt, der dieses ehemalige, zweigeschossige Warenhaus renovierte, wollte die existente Struktur bewahren, ohne die Fassaden zu verändern. So kam er auf die Idee, den Kontrast zwischen der vorhandenen Struktur und den hinzugefügten Elementen zu unterstreichen. Zunächst wurde die Struktur betont, indem man sie mit verspielten Formen und hellen Farben versah. So wurde ihre Präsenz hervorgehoben und die Aufmerksamkeit auf sie gelenkt. Außerdem sollte das Tageslicht so weit wie möglich ausgenutzt werden. Die Fassade wurde von allen Elementen befreit, die das Einfallen des Lichtes behinderten, und ein großes, rautenförmiges Fenster wurde geschaffen, das das Licht verteilt. Außerdem wurde der leere Raum unter der Treppe dazu benutzt, Tageslicht ins Innere dringen zu lassen.

The project has created an environment in which the placement of objects determines the use of each setting, so that functionality is closely linked to the visual effect.

Le projet a créé un environnement dans lequel l'emplacement des objets détermine la fonction de chaque espace. Fonctionnalité et impact visuel y sont étroitement liés.

Hier wurde eine Umgebung geschaffen, in der der Einsatz von Objekten die Nutzung der Räume bestimmt, so dass die Funktionalität eng mit der visuellen Wirkung verbunden ist.

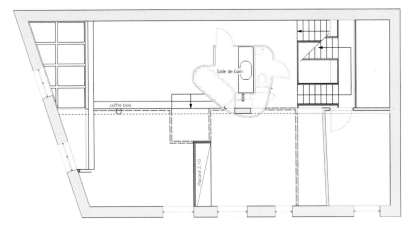

› Second floor   Deuxième étage   Zweite Obergeschoss

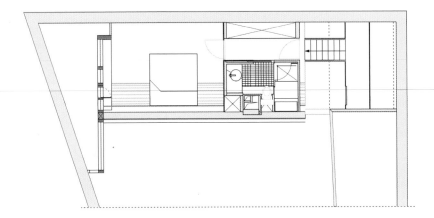

› First floor   Premier étage   Erstes Obergeschoss

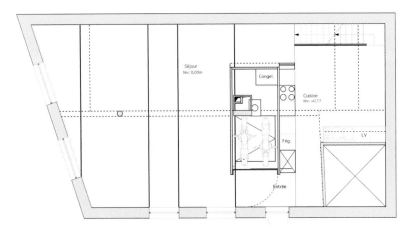

› Ground floor   Rez-de-chaussée   Erdgeschoss

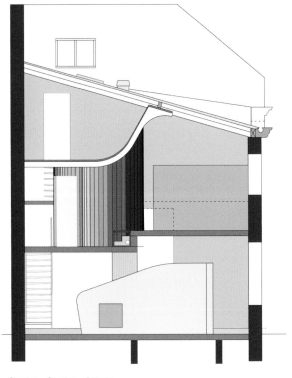

› Section   Section   Schnitt

...ne façade was stripped of any elements that impeded the flow of light and fitted with a large window, with an uneven shape designed to distribute light more effectively.

...a façade est libérée de tout élément gênant l'entrée de la lumière qu'elle peut mieux distribuer grâce à une grande fenêtre aux formes inégales.

...lle Elemente, die den Einfall des Lichtes behinderten, wurden von der Fassade entfernt und ein großes Fenster wurde geschaffen, das das Licht noch effektiver verteilt.

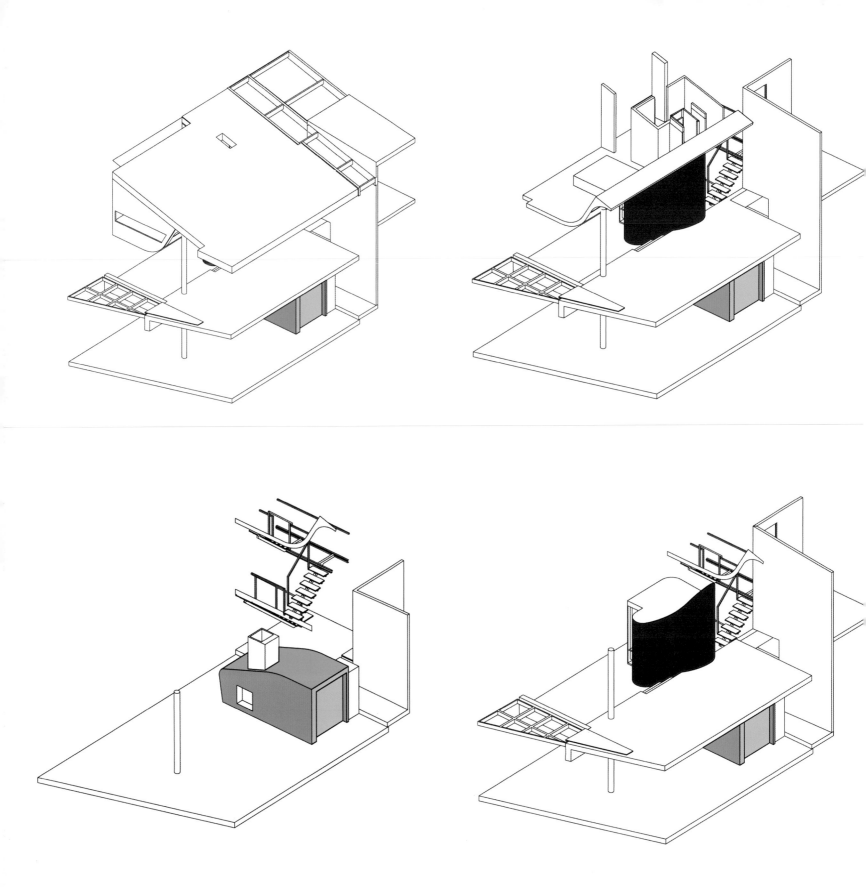

House inside a House
Maison dans une maison
Haus in Haus

Milan, Italy

Once the site of a big factory, this attic space was refurbished to create a living space for a young professional. The architectural elements, chosen for their contrasting volumes with respect to their function, establish the different areas within a fluid, open-plan space. The living room occupies the central area. A chimney that pierces the ceiling delineates the kitchen and dining area, which lie underneath a lowered ceiling that stops short on either side to receive a skylight. The vertical void above the kitchen is intersected by a glass panel that serves as a walkway on the attic level. A steel staircase leads to the bedroom, which is sheltered inside an independent structure for ultimate privacy and an escape from daily routine. Vintage and antique furniture mingle effortlessly with both ordinary and designer pieces, adding a great deal of character and personality to the home.

Cet espace sous les toits, jadis une ancienne usine, a été rénové pour devenir le logement d'un jeune professionnel. Les éléments architecturaux sélectionnés pour leurs volumes, alliant contraste et respect des fonctions, définissent les différentes zones selon un concept d'espace ouvert et fluide Le salon occupe la zone centrale. La cheminée perce le plafond et délimite ainsi la cuisine et la salle à manger située sous un plafond surbaissé, ouvert à chaque bout, pour laisser passer un puits de lumière. Le vide vertical au-dessus de la cuisine est interrompu par un panneau de verre qui sert de passage au niveau de la mansarde. Un escalier d'acier dessert la chambre protégée par une structure indépendante pour préserver l'intimité au maximum et rompre avec la routine quotidienne. Le mobilier ancien et classique s'unit parfaitement au meubles ordinaires ou design, exaltant à merveille le caractère et la personnalité de l'habitation.

Dieses Dachgeschoss, einst eine große Fabriketage, wurde zu einer Wohnung für ein junges Paar umgebaut. Die architektonischen Elemente, die aufgrund ihrer unterschiedlichen Volumen für die jeweiligen Funktionen gewählt wurden, bilden verschiedene Zonen in einem offenen Raum. Das Wohnzimmer befindet sich im Zentrum. Ein Kamin durchbohrt die Decke und begrenzt Küche und Essbereich, die unter einer abgehängten Decke liegen, in der sich auf beiden Seiten ein Oberlicht befindet. Der Hohlraum oberhalb der Küche wird von einer Glasplatte unterbrochen, die als Laufsteg der oberen Ebene dient. Eine Stahltreppe führt zum Schlafzimmer, das sich innerhalb einer unabhängigen Struktur befindet, ein Ort, um sich von der täglichen Routine zurückzuziehen. Alte, antike Möbel werden völlig ungezwungen mit außergewöhnlichen Elementen und Designermöbeln kombiniert, was diesem Zuhause einen ganz besonderen Charakter verleiht.

Lightweight elements like the minimal staircase and glass catwalk maintain the spacious character of this industrial loft.

Des éléments légers, à l'instar de l'escalier minimaliste et de la passerelle de verre, préservent l'espace de ce loft industriel.

Leichte Elemente wie die kleine Treppe und der Laufsteg aus Glas unterstreichen den weitläufigen Charakter dieser Fabriketage.

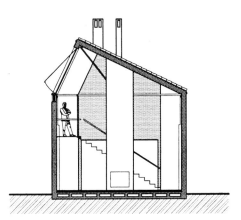

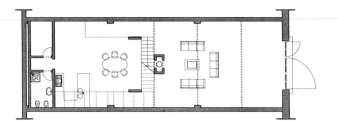

› Ground floor Rez-de-chaussée Erdgeschoss

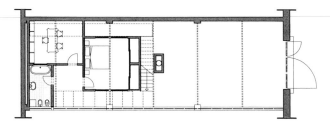

› First floor Premier étage Erstes Obergeschoss

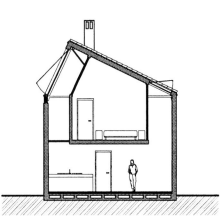

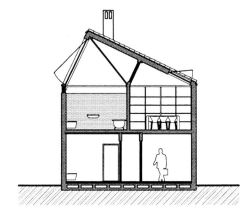

› Sections Sections Schnitte

The kitchen is both practical and attractive. Its U-shape allows for appliances to be kept out of sight of the living and dining area.

La cuisine décline commodité et beauté. Sa forme en U permet de maintenir les équipements hors de la vue de la salle à manger et du salon.

Die Küche ist praktisch und schön. In einer U-Form sind alle Geräte untergebracht, so dass sie vom Wohn- und Essbereich aus nicht sichtbar sind.

Loft in Pré Saint Gervais
Loft du Pré Saint Gervais
Loft in Pré Saint Gervais

Paris, France

This loft in France is the result of the conversion of an old factory into a bright residence, taking advantage of the great height and respecting the previous structure. In order to distribute the space, the project adopted the staircase as the central element to organize it on three levels and highlight the building's verticality. The stairs leading from the street level to the ground floor emerge from a painted concrete panel that sets off the lightness of the metal structure and the oak steps of the upper section leading to the first floor, as well as providing a visual separation between the living room and dining room. The materials used–metal and concrete–are simple, as is the parquet on the floor. The white walls enhance the feeling of spaciousness and intensify the natural light; bright colors were added to emphasize certain elements, such as the sliding panels, the closets, and the bookcase marking off the lower staircase.

Ce loft, situé en France, est le fruit de la transformation d'une ancienne usine en une grande résidence, tirant parti de la hauteur considérable tout en respectant la structure d'origine. Dans le projet, la structuration de l'espace s'articule autour d'un escalier central sur trois étages, soulignant ainsi la verticalité de l'édifice. L'escalier, partant du niveau de la rue vers le rez-de-chaussée, émerge au cœur d'un panneau de béton peint qui exalte la légèreté de sa structure en métal. Les marches du haut, en chêne, desservent le premier étage tout en créant une séparation visuelle entre le salon et la salle à manger. Les matériaux utilisés – métal et béton – sont simples comme le bois du parquet. Les murs blancs accentuent la sensation d'espace et font ressortir la lumière naturelle. Des couleurs vives rehaussent certains éléments, à l'instar des cloisons coulissantes, des placards et de la bibliothèque qui délimitent la partie basse de l'escalier.

Dieses Loft in Frankreich ist durch den Umbau einer alten Fabrik in eine helle Wohnung entstanden, wobei die Deckenhöhe und die bereits vorhandene Struktur bestens ausgenutzt wurde. Um den Raum zu unterteilen, wurde die Treppe als zentrales Element genommen, um das herum drei Ebenen geschaffen und die Vertikalität des Baus unterstrichen wurde. Die Treppe, die von der Straßenebene zum Erdgeschoss führt, entspringt einer gestrichenen Betonplatte, die die Leichtigkeit der Metallstruktur und der Eichenstufen, die zur ersten Etage führen, unterstreicht. Außerdem dient sie als visuelle Trennung zwischen dem Wohn- und Esszimmer. Die verwendeten Materialien, Metall und Beton, sind so einfach wie der Parkettboden. Die weißen Wände unterstreichen das Gefühl von Raum und Licht. Hinzu kommen helle Farben, die bestimmte Elemente wie die gleitenden Paneele, die Wandschränke und das Bücherregal am unteren Teil der Treppe hervorheben.

Materials like metal and concrete combine with the bright colors to enhance the feeling of spaciousness and intensify the natural light.

Métal et béton conjugués aux couleurs vives rehaussent la sensation d'espace et intensifient la lumière naturelle.

Durch Materialien wie Metall und Beton in Kombination mit hellen Farben wurde eine offene Atmosphäre geschaffen und das Tageslicht intensiviert.

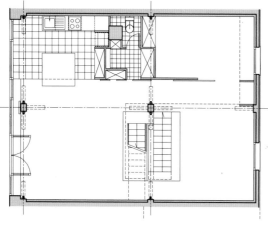

› First floor Premier étage Erstes Obergeschoss

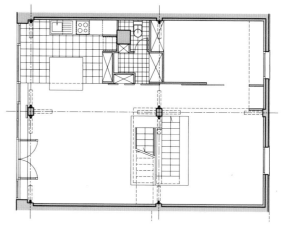

› Ground floor Rez-de-chaussée Erdgeschoss

208

Venice, Italy

Wagner Loft

This residence was inserted into an industrial shell that was originally built in 1910 and known as the Dreher Brewery. The architect's aim was to keep the structure intact by introducing new floors to hold up the rooms without removing any of the existing brick walls and wood trusses. The terraces and the lower level of the loft are raised by a suspended steel floor and a suspended steel frame wall, dividing the space from the rest of the surrounding structure. A stainless-steel staircase, consisting of single steps made of glass and steel sheets, guides the circulation throughout the space and ends up in the sleeping gallery, which contains a suspended, circular bath tub, a shower and a glass toilet cubicle. The wooden deck terrace is made up of paths and small ponds, providing an ideal place to relax and enjoy the views of Venice in the distance.

Le complexe industriel construit en 1910, connu sous le nom de Brasserie Dreher, abrite cette nouvelle résidence. L'architecte a voulu garder la structure préexistante. Il y a ajouté de nouveaux sols conservant ainsi les pièces sans toucher aux anciens murs de briques ni à la charpente de bois. Les terrasses et la partie inférieure du loft sont soutenues par un sol d'acier et un mur porteur suspendus, séparant l'espace du reste de la structure. Un escalier en acier inoxydable, constitué de marches individuelles en verre et feuilles d'aluminium, traverse l'espace pour aboutir à la galerie dortoir, dotée d'une baignoire circulaire suspendue, d'une douche et d'un lavabo de verre. La terrasse de bois est ponctuée de passages et de petits étangs, lieu idyllique pour se détendre et jouir des vues sur Venise qui se profile à l'horizon.

Dieses Wohnambiente befindet sich in der Dreher Brauerei, einem Industriegebäude aus dem Jahr 1910. Ziel des Architekten war es, die bestehende Struktur zu erhalten. Dazu konstruierte er neue Böden, die die Räume stützen, ohne dazu das existierende Fachwerk und die Ziegelwände entfernen zu müssen. Die Terrassen und das Erdgeschoss wurden auf einem aufgehängten Stahlboden und mit einer Wand aus Stahlrahmen konstruiert, und trennen den Raum von der umgebenden Struktur ab. Eine Edelstahltreppe, bestehend aus einzelnen Stufen aus Glas- und Stahlplatten, führt durch die Räume zur Schlafgalerie, in der sich eine aufgehängte, runde Badewanne, eine Dusche und eine Toilettenzelle aus Glas befinden. Über die holzbelegte Dachterrasse führen Pfade und kleine Brücken und sie dient, als idealer Ort zum Entspannen, von dem aus man Venedig in der Ferne sieht.

The asymmetrical fireplace and supporting steel columns are some of the various sculptural elements that give character to the home.

La cheminée asymétrique et les colonnes portantes en acier sont quelques-uns des éléments sculpturaux qui caractérisent ce lieu.

Der asymmetrische Kamin und die Stützsäulen aus Stahl sind einige der verschiedenen, skulpturalen Elemente, die diesem Zuhause einen besonderen Charakter verleihen.

› **Ground floor** Rez-de-chaussée Erdgeschoss   › **First floor** Premier étage Erstes Obergeschoss   › **Second floor** Deuxième étage Zweite Obergeschoss   › **Section** Section Schnitt

On the top floor, a free-standing shower separates the bedroom from the bathroom area.

A l'étage supérieur, une douche autoportante sépare la chambre de la salle de bains.

Im Obergeschoss trennt eine freistehende Dusche das Schlafzimmer vom Badezimmer ab.

The exterior of this house, which reflects its industrial origins, has been transformed into an Italian villa with the help of a meticulously landscaped garden.

L'extérieur de cette maison, qui reflète ses origines industrielles, a été transformé en une villa italienne grâce à un remodelage méticuleux du jardin.

Von außen verlieh man diesem Haus, dem man seine industriellen Ursprünge noch ansieht, durch einen sorgfältig gestalteten Garten das Flair einer italienischen Villa.

Loft in Brooklyn
Loft à Brooklyn
Loft in Brooklyn

New York, United States

This former warehouse was converted into a church in the 1930s. The architects bought the neglected property and transformed it into a home for a family of four. The space was gutted, although even the shell was in need of repair. Major structural work included rebuilding an exterior wall and bolstering existing trusses with new heavy-timber struts and steel plates. In order to emphasize the immense two-story volume, a series of deep skylights was installed into the ceiling to flood the space with light. The industrial character of the space was maintained, leaving the new masonry wall exposed and painting the stripped floors. The mezzanine, once the church's choir stalls, contains an intimate living area and shelters another lounge underneath, offering cozy alternatives to the main room. The stainless-steel kitchen is a welcome contrast to the loft's wooden framework.

Dans les années 30, cet ancien entrepôt a été reconverti en église. Après l'achat de cette propriété délaissée, les architectes l'ont restructurée en résidence pour une famille de quatre personnes. L'espace était vide et l'ossature même devait d'être réparée. Il fallut entreprendre de sérieux travaux de structure, notamment reconstruire l'extérieur et renforcer les poutres existantes par de nouveaux arcs-boutants de bois et des plaques d'acier. Pour mettre en valeur ce volume réparti sur deux étages, une série de velux a été installée dans le toit inondant ainsi l'espace de lumière. Grâce au nouveau mur en maçonnerie brute et aux sols striés peints, ce bâtiment conserve son cachet de bâtiment industriel. La mezzanine, à l'emplacement des anciennes stalles d'église, est dotée d'une salle de séjour et abrite un autre salon en dessous, une alternative conviviale et confortable à la pièce principale. La cuisine en inox contraste agréablement avec la charpente de bois du loft.

Dieses ehemalige Warenhaus wurde 1930 in eine Kirche umgewandelt. Die Architekten kauften den vernachlässigten Besitz und schufen ein Zuhause für eine vierköpfige Familie. Das Haus wurde von innen ausgenommen, obwohl sogar die Fassade reparaturbedürftig war. Zu diesen großen Strukturarbeiten gehörten der Wiederaufbau der Außenmauer und das Stützen des orignalen Hängewerks. Um die Höhe des zweistöckigen Raumes zu unterstreichen, strömt Sonnenlicht durch eine Reihe tiefer Dachfenster in alle Winkel. Der industrielle Charakter des Gebäudes blieb erhalten, die neugemauerte Wand blieb unverputzt und die freigelegten Fußböden wurden gestrichen. Im Zwischengeschoss, wo einst der Chor der Kirche war, entstand ein intimer Wohnbereich und darunter ein anderes Wohnzimmer, so dass man über zwei gemütliche Gesellschaftszimmer verfügt. Die Küche aus Edelstahl bildet einen angenehmen Gegensatz zu den Holzbalken.

A series of deep skylights were installed into the ceiling to allow light to spill into the space, while the room was furnished with a giant 20-ft table and long bookcases.

Une série de grands velux a été installée dans le plafond pour permettre à la lumière d'inonder l'espace. La pièce est dotée d'une table géante de 6 mètres de long et d'une bibliothèque tout en longueur.

Es wurden eine Reihe von tiefen Dachfenstern in der Decke installiert, so dass der ganze Raum, der mit einem riesigen, 6 m langen Tisch und langen Bücherregalen möbliert ist, von Tageslicht überflutet wird.

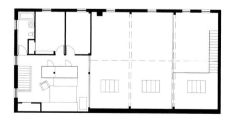

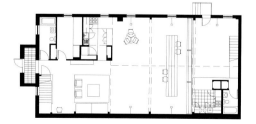

› First floor   Premier étage   Erstes Obergeschoss

› Ground floor   Rez-de-chaussée   Erdgeschoss

› Basement   Sous-sol   Kellergeschoss

Loft on Rue Huyghens
Loft de la rue Huyghens
Loft in der Rue Huyghens

aris, France

This project sought to take the fullest possible dvantage of sunlight, provide more space, and pen up the field of vision. These aims were fulfied by knocking down walls and reducing the surace area of the first floor to expose the full height f the large window opening on to the courtyard. spiral staircase–rescued from an old spinning ill–links the two levels, freeing the entrance and earing up as an almost sculptural element that akes it possible to modulate the space. The brary-living room and the kitchen are situated ell apart, at either end of the ground floor, to nsure a clear separation between the settings. he upper floor contains, on one side, the main edroom and, on the other, two smaller ones. The all dividing the main bedroom from the rest has een left with three translucent vertical openings at make it visually less heavy.

Le but du projet était de tirer profit au maximum de la lumière du jour, d'agrandir l'espace et d'ouvrir le champ visuel. Il a donc fallu abattre les murs et réduire la surface au sol du premier étage pour mettre en valeur la hauteur de la grande fenêtre ouverte sur la cour. Un escalier hélicoïdal – récupéré dans un vieil atelier de tissage – relie les deux niveaux, libérant l'entrée et s'élançant comme une sculpture qui module l'espace. La séparation nette entre le salon bibliothèque et la cuisine, aux deux extrémités du rez-de-chaussée, instaure une réelle division de l'espace. L'étage supérieur comprend, d'un côté, la chambre à coucher principale, de l'autre, deux plus petites. Le mur séparant la chambre principale du reste est percé d'ouvertures verticales translucides pour une légèreté visuelle accrue.

Durch die Planung dieses Lofts wurden das Tageslicht und der vorhandene Raum optimal ausgenutzt und die Aussicht deutlich verbessert. Dazu wurden einige Wände entfernt und die erste Etage verkleinert, so dass man die volle Höhe des großen Fensters sehen kann, das zum Hof geht. Eine Wendeltreppe aus einer alten Spinnerei verbindet die beiden Ebenen, schafft Platz am Eingang und wirkt wie ein skulpturelles Element, das den Raum gestaltet. Das kombinierte Wohnzimmer/Bibliothek und die Küche befinden sich weit voneinander entfernt an den Enden des Erdgeschosses, so dass es eine klare Trennung dieser beiden Bereiche gibt. Auf der oberen Etage liegen auf einer Seite das Hauptschlafzimmer und auf der anderen Seite zwei kleinere Schlafräume. Die Wand, die das Hauptschlafzimmer von den anderen trennt, besitzt drei vertikale, lichtdurchlässige Öffnungen, die sie visuell leichter wirken lässt.

A large window on the façade opening on to the courtyard allows natural light to flow in and penetrate the whole living area.

Une grande baie vitrée sur la façade qui s'ouvre sur l'atrium, laisse la lumière naturelle inonder le salon.

Durch ein großes Fenster zum Hof strömt reichlich Tageslicht in die Räume und durchdringt den gesamten Wohnbereich.

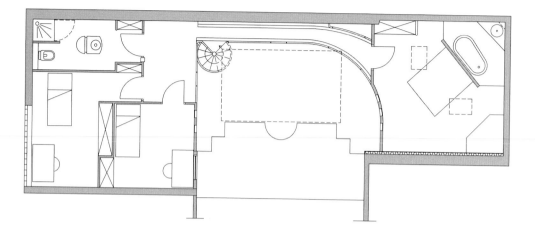

› **Ground floor** Rez-de-chaussée Erdgeschoss

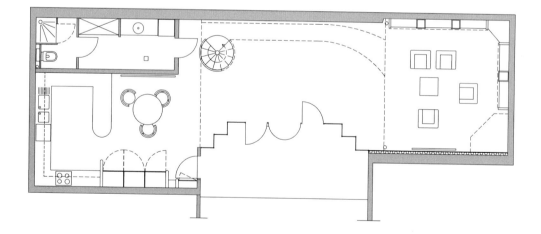

› **First floor** Premier étage Erstes Obergeschoss

Taffer Loft

New York, United States

Audrey Matlock Architects restored one floor of an industrial complex on the shore of the Hudson River, and converted it into a home for a couple. As the clients did not require too intimate a space, the project envisioned a house with an open layout. Although the different areas are sometimes divided, they always maintain a certain relationship with one another, thanks to mobile partitions. Some of these are partially translucent, as they are inset with a glass upper section, while others do not reach the ceiling and consist of wooden or treated glass panels set within a steel frame and fitted with wheels that slide along rails in the ceiling or floor. The concrete structure has been preserved and is visible in the ceilings and columns. As an esthetic counterpoint, some of the walls were painted white and others were covered with maple wood.

Le bureau d'architectes Audrey Matlock a restauré l'étage d'un complexe industriel sur les berges de la rivière Hudson et l'a converti en un logement pour un couple. A la requête des clients, peu axés sur l'intimité, la maison a été conçue comme un espace ouvert. Même si les différentes zones sont parfois divisées, elles gardent toujours une certaine corrélation, grâce à des cloisons amovibles. Certaines d'entre elles sont translucides, dotées d'une partie supérieure en verre, d'autres ne vont pas jusqu'au plafond et sont faites de panneaux en bois ou en verre traité, insérés dans un cadre de métal monté sur roulettes et glissant dans un rail fixé au plafond ou au sol. Le béton est conservé et visible sur les colonnes ou au plafond. Points d'orgue esthétiques, certains murs sont peints en blanc ou habillés de bois d'érable.

Audrey Matlock Architects setzten eine Etage eines Industriegebäudes am Ufer des Hudson Rivers instand und machten daraus ein Zuhause für ein Ehepaar. Da die Kunden sich keine allzu intimen Räume wünschten, wurde das Haus sehr offen angelegt. Obwohl die verschiedenen Bereiche teilweise unterteilt sind, stehen sie immer zueinander in Beziehung, da die Trennelemente beweglich sind. Einige davon sind durch den Einsatz von Glasstreifen imdoeren Bereich lichtdurchlässig. Andere reichen bis zur Decke und bestehen aus Holz- oder behandelten Glasplatten in einem Stahlrahmen auf Rädern, die über Schienen im Boden und an der Decke verschoben werden. Die Betonstruktur blieb erhalten und ist in der Decke und den Säulen noch sichtbar. Um einen ästhetischen Kontrapunkt zu schaffen, sind einige der Wände weiß gestrichen und andere mit Ahornholz verkleidet.

A motorized system of lightweight white drapes offers intimacy and regulates the entrance of natural light; they can be taken down and hidden behind the radiators.

Un système de tentures légères et blanches, à commande électrique, permet de créer une certaine intimité et de régler le flux de lumière naturelle. Démontables, elles sont faciles à dissimuler derrière les radiateurs.

Durch ein motorisiertes System aus leichten, weißen Stoffen können die Räume abgeteilt und das Einfallen des Tageslichts reguliert werden. Die Stoffe können ganz heruntergelassen und hinter den Heizkörpern verborgen werden.

› Plan Plan Grundriss

The enormous windows in the kitchen provide ample light and magnificent views of the surroundings. The small table serves for informal meals and breakfasts.

Les immenses baies vitrées de la cuisine permettent à la lumière d'entrée en abondance et offrent des vues splendides sur les alentours. La petite table sert aux repas et petits déjeuners en famille.

Die Küchenfenster sind riesig, so dass viel Licht einfällt und man einen wundervollen Blick auf die Umgebung hat. Der kleine Tisch wird zum Frühstücken und anderen zwanglosen Mahlzeiten benutzt.

Loft in Prenzlauer Berg
Loft á Prenzlauer Berg
Loft im Prenzlauer Berg

Berlin, Germany

Four young people rented this loft in the Prenzlauer Berg neighborhood, formerly part of East Berlin, and converted it into their home. It is set in an old post office building that had been abandoned for five years. The old administrative offices on the first floor were divided into four private rooms, a large communal space with a kitchen and living room, and a multipurpose hall with ranks of bookshelves and a dining room. The interior decoration took full advantage of the existing fittings and party walls. A tight budget can sometimes lead to poorly designed and uninviting spaces; in this case, imagination and ingenuity more than compensated for any shortage of money and the result is a warm, comfortable home. The lamps, for example, consist of old luminous signs, while the furniture is an amusing mix of secondhand or recycled objects, such as the bed with a base of bricks covered with a wooden plank.

Quatre jeunes ont loué ce loft à Prenzlauer Berg - ancien quartier de Berlin Est - dans une vieille poste abandonnée depuis cinq ans, pour y élire domicile. Les anciens bureaux administratifs, au premier étage, ont été divisés en quatre parties privées, un vaste espace commun doté d'une cuisine et d'un salon, un hall d'entrée polyvalent garni d'étagères et une salle à manger. L'agencement existant et les cloisons initiales ont servi de base à la décoration intérieure. En général, les budgets serrés ne sont pas synonymes d'espaces design et accueillants. Dans ce cas précis et en dépit des faibles moyens, le mariage de l'ingéniosité et de l'imagination a réussi à créer un logement confortable et chaleureux. Les lampes, par exemple, sont d'anciennes enseignes lumineuses, l'ameublement est un méli-mélo sympathique d'objets d'occasion ou recyclés, à l'instar du lit fait d'un socle de briques recouvert d'une planche de bois.

Vier junge Menschen mieteten dieses Loft am Prenzlauer Berg, ehemals Ostberlin, um es in ihr Zuhause zu verwandeln. Es befindet sich in einem alten, seit fünf Jahren leer stehenden Postgebäude. Die ehemalige Post im Erdgeschoss wurde in vier private Räume, einen großen Gemeinschaftsraum mit Küche und Wohnzimmer, einen Mehrzweckraum mit Bücherregalen und ein Esszimmer unterteilt. Bei der Innengestaltung wurden die existierenden Verbindungen und Wände einbezogen. Wenn wenig Geld zur Verfügung steht, führt dies manchmal zu ärmlich wirkenden, ungemütlichen Räumen. In diesem Fall aber wurde dieser Mangel an finanziellen Mitteln durch einen immensen Einfallsreichtum wettgemacht, so dass ein warmes und gastliches Zuhause entstand. Die Lampen zum Beispiel sind alte Leuchtreklamen, das Mobiliar ist eine amüsante Mischung aus Objekten aus zweiter Hand und recycelten Elementen wie dem Bett mit einer Basis aus Ziegelsteinen und einer Holzplatte.

The combination of different types of furniture and decorative elements (antiques, secondhand pieces, paintings and prints, and luminous signs) makes for an eclectic and warm setting.

L'alliance de différentes sortes de meubles et divers éléments de décoration (antiquités, meubles d'occasion, peintures, gravures et enseignes lumineuses) engendre un agencement aussi chaleureux qu'éclectique.

Die Kombination verschiedener Möbeltypen und Dekorationselemente (Antiquitäten, Gegenstände aus zweiter Hand, Gemälde, Drucke und Leuchtschilder) lässt das Loft eklektisch und warm wirken.

Loft in Lombardia
Loft à Lombardia
Loft in Lombardia

Milan, Italy

The studio BauQ transformed this 1920's industrial warehouse into a home for an artist, a textile designer and their daughter. The elongated shape of the space and its high ceilings impelled the architects to divide it lengthwise and create a mezzanine that serves as a studio. A half-height white panel was used for this purpose, ensuring a visual continuity within the space and avoiding a rigid separation between the two areas. A metal grated staircase leads up to the studio, which was made with prefabricated white cement slabs laid over a metal structure. Beyond the stairs and a translucent screen, the kitchen and dining area share a common space, which leads on to the daughter's bedroom. A full-height window fills the lively and playful room with natural light during the day. The framework of wooden beams on the roof structure is the most notable architectural feature of the loft and dates back to the 1950s.

Le studio BauQ a transformé cet entrepôt industriel des années 20, en une maison d'artiste, pour un designer textile et sa fille. La forme allongée de l'espace et ses hauts plafonds ont amené les architectes à le diviser dans le sens de la longueur et de créer une mezzanine qui serve de studio. Un panneau blanc à mi-hauteur permet une continuité visuelle au cœur de l'espace, évitant la séparation stricte des deux zones. Un escalier de métal grillagé conduit au studio, réalisé en placoplâtre posé sur une ossature de métal. Cachés derrière l'escalier et un paravent translucide, la cuisine et la salle à manger se partagent l'espace qui mène à la chambre de la fille. Une fenêtre, couvrant toute la hauteur, inonde de lumière du jour la pièce gaie et ludique. La charpente en bois, des années 50, est le plus bel élément architectural, image de marque du loft.

Das Studio BauQ baute dieses Lagerhaus aus den Zwanzigerjahren in ein Heim für eine Künstlerfamilie (Künstler, Textildesigner und Tochter) um. Der lange Raum mit den hohen Decken brachte den Architekten auf die Idee, ihn der Länge nach aufzuteilen und ein Zwischengeschoss zu schaffen, das als Atelier dient. Dazu wurde ein weißes Paneel halber Höhe benutzt, so dass die visuelle Kontinuität des Raumes bewahrt wurde, da keine starre Trennung der beiden Bereiche notwendig war. Eine Treppe aus Metallgitter führt zum Atelier, das aus vorgefertigten Zementplatten über einer Metallstruktur konstruiert wurde. Hinter der Treppe und einem lichtdurchlässigen Schirm teilen sich Küche und Essbereich den Raum, der zum Schlafzimmer der Tochter führt. Ein deckenhohes Fenster lässt das Tageslicht in diesen lebendigen und verspielten Raum strömen. Das interessanteste architektonische Element dieses Lofts ist das Holzfachwerk des Daches aus den Fünfzigerjahren.

Brick pillars mark the transition from public to private areas. Just behind, a metal grated staircase leads to the artist's studio.

Des colonnes de briques délimitent les zones privées et publiques entre elles. Juste derrière, un escalier en grille métallique mène au studio de l'artiste.

Ziegelsteinsäulen markieren den Übergang von den öffentlichen zu den privaten Bereichen. Genau dahinter führt eine Treppe aus Metallgitter zum Künstleratelier.

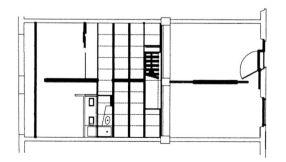

› Ground floor Rez-de-chaussée Erdgeschoss

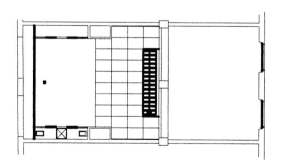

› First floor Premier étage Erstes Obergeschoss

› Section Section Schnitt

The most notable architectural feature of the loft is the framework of wooden beams, which is completed with a skylight that enables sunshine to penetrate within the space.

La structure de la charpente du toit en poutres de bois, complétée par un velux qui permet au soleil d'inonder l'espace, est l'élément architectural le plus remarquable du loft.

Das bemerkenswerteste Element dieses Loft ist das Holzfachwerk der Dachstruktur, in der ein Oberlicht angebracht wurde, durch das die Sonne in den Raum dringt.

Hill Loft

New York, United States

This New York loft is an example of an efficient response to the problem of limited space in the refurbishment of this small urban dwelling, with simplicity being the key factor. The wall running along the kitchen, lounge-dining room, and bedroom was completely fitted with closets and shelves, while steel columns were inserted to visually separate these three areas. In the center of the kitchen area, a sculptural rectangular island incorporates the table for eating, the range and the bar. A flexible tube with lights inside cuts across the entire loft from the entrance to cast light throughout. A sense of expansiveness is created in this reduced space by using pale colors and whites combined with wood tones, which also add warmth.

La rénovation de ce petit logement urbain, un loft à New York, montre comment résoudre efficacement le problème d'espace. Le mur longeant la cuisine, le salon-salle à manger et les chambres est entièrement aménagé de placards et d'étagères. L'insertion de colonnes d'acier crée une séparation visuelle des ces trois zones. Au centre de la zone cuisine, un îlot sculptural rectangulaire englobe la table, les rangements et le bar. Un tube flexible, avec un éclairage intégré, traverse tout le loft depuis l'entrée pour l'inonder de lumière. Les couleurs pales et les nuances de blanc, associées à des tons boisés, agrandissent cet espace réduit et y ajoutent une touche de chaleur.

In diesem Loft in New York wurde das Platzproblem hervorragend gelöst. Durch die Sanierung entstand eine kleine, einfach gehaltene Wohneinheit. Die Wand, die an der Küche, dem kombinierten Wohn- und Esszimmer und dem Schlafzimmer entlang führt, wurde vollständig mit Wandschränken und Regalen versehen. Die drei Bereiche sind visuell durch Stahlsäulen getrennt. In der Küchenmitte befindet sich eine skulpturell wirkende, rechteckige Insel, die als Esstisch, Arbeitsfläche und Bar dient. Ein im Inneren mit Leuchten versehenes, flexibles Rohr beginnt am Eingang und verläuft durch das ganze Loft, so wird überall Licht verteilt. Durch blasse und weiße Töne in Kombination mit den Farben des Holzes wirken die kleinen Räume bedeutend größer, und sehr einladend.

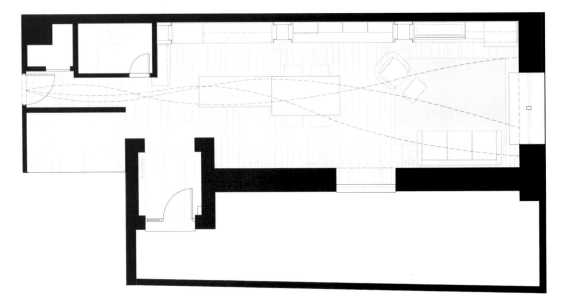

› Plan Plan Grundriss

Frank + Amy

New York, United States

These premises in the center of New York occupy an entire floor of an old industrial building and were designed for a film critic and an editor. The large windows with dynamic views of the city play a key role in the division of the space. The conceptual approach to the construction enhances the industrial atmosphere and converts it into a sculptural intervention in the pre-existing space. The result is a complex, compact cube that separates the public and private areas and becomes the structural axis of the space. The use of different materials was determined by the abundant light in the loft. Different types of woods were used to create a harmonious and warm atmosphere. The pipes and ducts for the electrical installation and heating were left uncovered on the ceiling, serving as decoration and recalling the building's functional, industrial past.

Ce logement au centre de New York, occupant l'étage entier d'un vieux bâtiment industriel, a été conçu pour un critique de film et un éditeur. Les grandes fenêtres avec vue panoramique sur la cité jouent un rôle clé dans la division de l'espace. L'approche conceptuelle de la construction souligne l'atmosphère industrielle de l'espace préexistant tout en lui conférant une allure sculpturale. Il en résulte un cube compact et complexe qui sépare les zones privées et publiques et devient l'axe structural de l'espace. L'abondance de lumière dans le loft a été un critère décisif dans le choix des matériaux. L'atmosphère harmonieuse et chaude est le fruit de différentes essences de bois. Au plafond, les tuyaux et conduits de l'installation électrique et du chauffage sont apparents. Devenus éléments de décoration, ils ne sont pas sans rappeler le passé industriel de l'édifice.

Diese Wohnung wurde in einer Fabriketage eines alten Gebäudes in New York geschaffen, sie gehört einem Filmkritiker und einer Editorin. Das große Fenster mit einem tollen Blick auf die City spielt eine Schlüsselrolle in der Raumaufteilung. Die konzeptuelle Herangehensweise an das Projekt unterstreicht die industrielle Atmosphäre und wird zu einem skulpturellen Eingriff in einen bereits existierenden Raum. Das Ergebnis ist ein komplexer und kompakter Würfel, der die öffentlichen von den privaten Bereichen trennt und zur strukturellen Achse der Räume wird. Durch die Verwendung unterschiedlicher Materialien erhält das Loft sehr viel Licht. Mit verschiedenen Holzarten wurde eine harmonische und warme Atmosphäre geschaffen. Die Rohre und Leitungen der elektrischen Installationen und der Heizung verlaufen sichtbar auf der Decke. Sie dienen als Dekoration und erinnern an die funktionelle und industrielle Vergangenheit des Gebäudes.

The space is organized around a cube, which distributes the space by separating and the various spaces in different directions.

L'espace s'articule autour d'un cube qui le distribue en séparant diverses zones dans des directions différentes.

Um eine Würfelform herum wurden die Räume unterteilt und in verschiedene Richtungen organisiert.

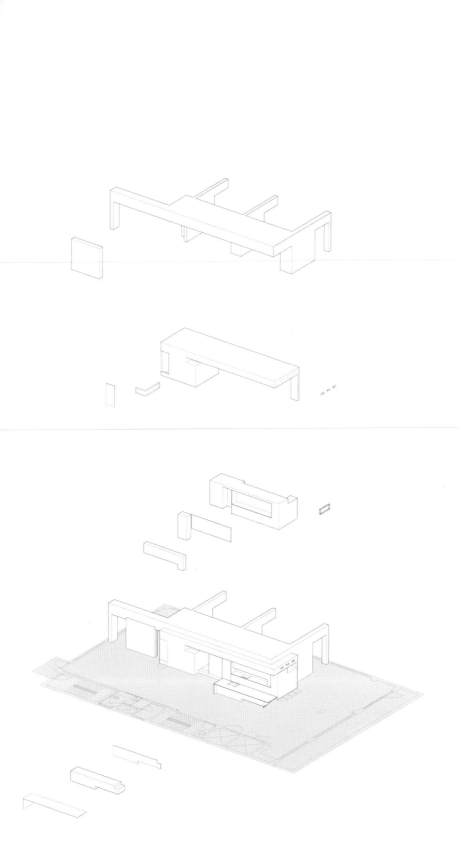

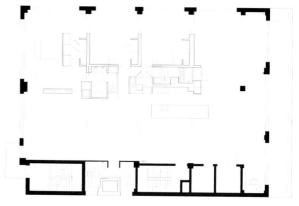

› Plan Plan Grundriss

258

Barbieri Loft

London, United Kingdom

The limited dimensions of these premises on the second floor of a 19th-century industrial building served for the Simon Conder studio to create living quarters and an office for a journalist and a photographer. The objective was to create spacious and bright settings that were well communicated with each other–particularly in the case of the kitchen and the living room, to facilitate the conversation between those who are cooking and their guests. Moreover, ample storage space was required, and the studio had to be separated from the living quarters. A crucial decision was made to create a single setting, organized by means of mobile partitions, rather than subdividing the space into different rooms. A large unit was installed to house the kitchen and the bathroom. The latter comprises three separate modules: the sink, the toilet and the shower, but if the doors at both ends are pushed back, the three areas become a single room.

Le deuxième étage, aux dimensions restreintes, au cœur d'un bâtiment industriel du XIXe siècle, a été transformé par le studio Simon Conder, en espace habitable et en bureau pour un journaliste et un photographe. Le but était de créer des espaces généreux et lumineux communicants entre eux - notamment la cuisine et le salon living room, pour faciliter la conversation entre la personne à la cuisine et les invités. Toutefois, face au besoin de rangements, le studio a dû être séparé des pièces à vivre. Les concepteurs ont opté pour la création d'un espace unique, organisé autour de partitions modulables, plutôt que de diviser l'espace en plusieurs pièces. Une unité spacieuse englobe la cuisine et une salle de bains. Cette dernière comprend trois modules séparés, le lavabo, les toilettes et la douche qui se transforment en une seule pièce, en repoussant les portes à chaque extrémité.

Conder Studio schufen in diesen relativ kleinen Räumen in der zweiten Etage eines Industriegebäudes aus dem 19. Jh. Wohn- und Arbeitsbereiche für ein Paar (Journalist und Fotograf). Es sollte eine weite und helle Umgebung entstehen, und alle Räume sollten miteinander verbunden sein, vor allem die Küche und das Wohnzimmer, damit während des Kochens eine Unterhaltung mit den Gästen stattfinden kann. Es war auch viel Abstellraum notwendig, und das Studio sollte von den Wohnräumen abgetrennt sein. Entscheidend bei der Planung war es, dass ein einziger Raum mit mobilen Abteilungen geschaffen wurde, anstatt ihn in verschiedene Zimmer zu unterteilen. Es wurde ein große Einheit installiert, in der sich Küche und Bad befinden. Das Bad besteht aus drei separaten Modulen, Waschbecken, Toilette und Dusche, aber wenn man die Türen auf beiden Seiten öffnet, wird daraus ein einziger Raum.

The furniture is custom-made for the project and comes with a lighting system incorporated into the ends of the surfaces.

Le mobilier a été dessiné sur mesure y compris le système d'éclairage intégré aux extrémités des surfaces.

Die Möbel sind auf Maß gearbeitet und mit einem eingebauten Beleuchtungssystem ausgestattet.

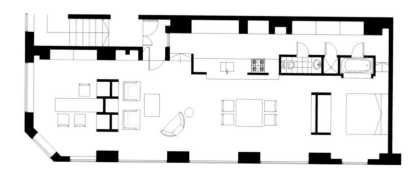

› Plan Plan Grundriss

The bathroom continues the theme of the furniture by using wood, except for the sides of the shower, which are made of panes of translucent glass.

Dans la ligne du mobilier, la salle de bains utilise le bois à l'exception des panneaux de verre translucide de la douche.

Der Stil des Mobiliars wird im Badezimmer fortgesetzt, wo Holz benutzt wurde. Nur die Seiten der Duschkabine sind aus lichtdurchlässigem Glas.

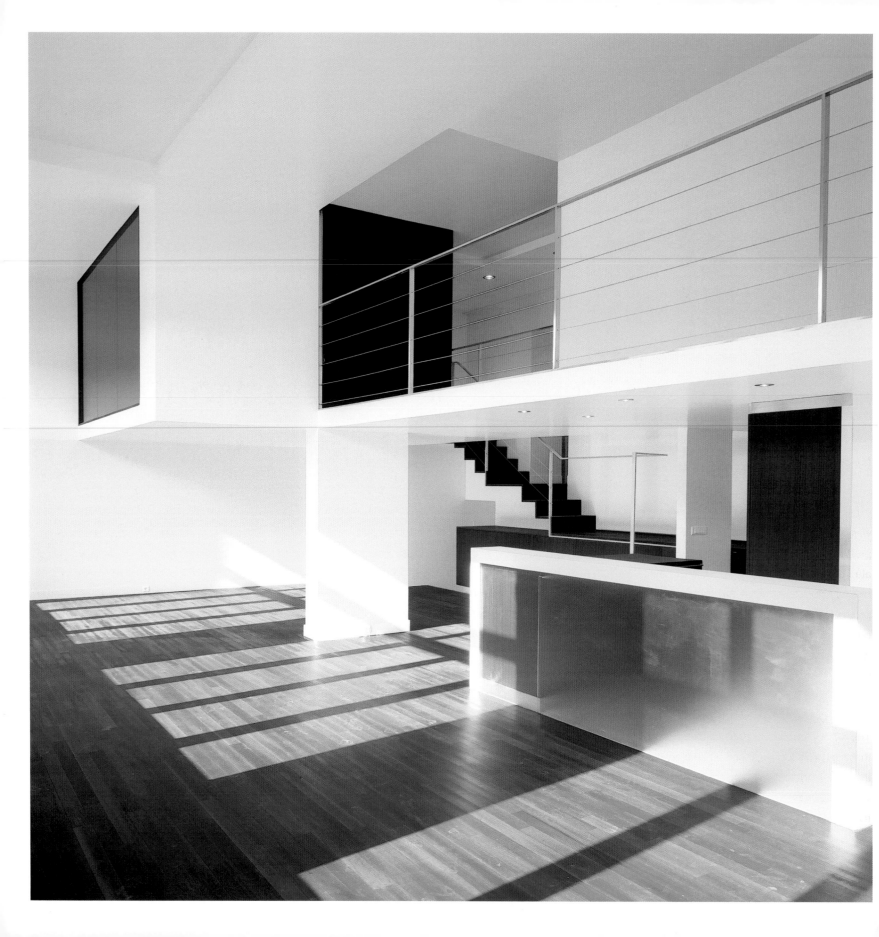

Loft in Montrouge
Loft à Montrouge
Loft in Montrouge

Montrouge, France

In this project, the architect Jean-Pierre Lévêque was able to take advantage of the volume and light provided by a 19th-century factory building, to create a home spread over four levels with a configuration that differed from the original layout. The project set up an interplay between containers and contents, an intelligent puzzle dominated by continuity; the insertion of autonomous elements in some areas provides intimacy and the feeling of being either inside or outside. The cube shapes and straight lines flow smoothly into one another. The distribution was designed to attain a continuity that makes it possible to go up to the next level and then return below without straying from a single path. This was achieved with a specific program that designed the spaces independently of the functions that they would take on. These functions were adapted to the project afterwards, as the system made it possible to define the use that would be given to each space with geometrical precision.

Pour ce projet, l'architecte Jean-Pierre Lévêque a su tirer parti du volume et de la lumière de cette usine du XIXe siècle, pour créer un logement organisé sur quatre étages, d'après un plan différent de l'original. Ce projet se base sur l'interaction entre les contenants et leur contenu. C'est un puzzle bien pensé sous le signe de la continuité. L'intégration, à certains endroits, d'éléments autonomes favorise l'intimité et la sensation de n'être ni exclu, ni enfermé. Les formes et lignes droites du cube se fondent en douceur l'une à l'autre. La conception de l'organisation de l'espace s'inscrit dans la continuité ce qui permet de passer d'un niveau à l'autre en suivant le même chemin. Ceci a été possible grâce à un programme spécifique concevant les espaces indépendamment de leurs fonctions. Le rôle de chaque pièce a été défini plus tard, grâce à ce système permettant d'attribuer la fonction à chaque espace avec une précision d'horloger.

Der Architekt Jean-Pierre Lévêque nutzte bei der Planung dieses Lofts die Formen und das Licht in dem Fabrikgebäude aus dem 19. Jh. aus, um eine Wohnung auf vier Ebenen zu schaffen, die sich von der ursprünglichen Anordnung unterscheidet. Das Projekt stellt eine Art Wechselspiel zwischen dem Behälter und Inhalt dar, ein intelligentes Puzzle, dessen Hauptcharakterzug die Kontinuität ist. Durch das Einfügen autonomer Elemente in einige Bereiche wird Privatsphäre geschaffen und das Gefühl, sich innen oder außen zu befinden. Die geraden Formen und Linien der Würfel gehen sanft ineinander über. Durch diese Verteilung wurde eine Kontinuität erreicht, durch die man auf dem gleichen Weg nach oben und unten gehen kann. Dies wurde erreicht, indem man die Räume unabhängig von ihrer Funktion gestaltete. Diese Funktionen wurden später an die Planung angepasst. Das System machte es möglich, die Benutzung der Räume mit geometrischer Genauigkeit zu definieren.

The used materials underline the general concept: the parquet, made of maçaranduba wood, helps to unify the space, while the stainless steel on the staircase lightens it up.

Les matériaux employés soulignent le concept général : le parquet, en bois de macaranduba unifie l'espace que la rampe en acier inoxydable de l'escalier rehausse.

Durch den gezielten Einsatz bestimmter Materialien wurde das grundlegende Konzept noch unterstrichen. Das Massaranduba-Parkett vereinheitlicht den Raum, und der Edelstahl des Handlaufs der Treppe macht ihn heller.

› Ground floor Rez-de-chaussée Erdgeschoss

› First floor Premier étage Erstes Obergeschoss

The various spaces were first designed independently of their functions to form an intelligent puzzle dominated by the theme of continuity.

Au départ, les différents espaces ont été conçus indépendamment de leurs fonctions pour former un puzzle astucieux régit par l'idée de continuité.

Bei der Gestaltung der verschiedenen Räume wurde zunächst deren Funktion außer Betracht gelassen. So entstand ein intelligentes Puzzle, dessen Grundlage die Kontinuität ist.

Loft on Rue Arthur Rozier
Loft de la rue Arthur Rozier
Loft in der Rue Arthur Rozier

Paris, France

In order to take maximum advantage of the height of this old print shop in Paris, the architect Alessandro Mosca divided the space horizontally and drew up a mezzanine that is accessed by two different stretches of staircase. The configuration of the staircase, the loft's central element, leads to the unusual layout of the upper floor: to one side, the bedroom and the studio; on the other, the bathroom. This also facilitates an interesting distribution of the spaces on the ground floor. As the building's structure is very old, the mezzanine was supported by an independent structure. Moreover, it does not occupy the overall surface area but pulls back slightly to allow light to pour in from the courtyard through the windows and the skylights. The conversion uses simple, cheap and resistant materials, while the decoration establishes a contrast between the dominant pale colors on the walls and a scattering of bright red elements.

Pour optimiser la hauteur de cette ancienne imprimerie parisienne, l'architecte Alessandro Mosca a divisé l'espace horizontalement et a installé une mezzanine accessible par deux escaliers différents. La configuration de l'escalier, élément central du loft, mène à l'étage supérieur conçu de manière inhabituelle : la chambre à coucher et le studio, d'un côté et la salle de bains, de l'autre. Au rez-de-chaussée, la distribution de l'espace est, également originale. Vu l'ancienneté de l'ossature de l'édifice, une structure indépendante a été installée pour soutenir la mezzanine. Toutefois, elle ne couvre pas toute la surface mais s'inscrit légèrement en retrait, permettant à la lumière de la cour de pénétrer par les fenêtres et les velux. Des matériaux bon marché et résistants ont été employés lors de la restauration. Sur le plan décoratif, les couleurs pâles qui dominent les murs contrastent avec les taches rouge vif de quelques éléments épars.

Um die Höhe dieser ehemaligen Druckerei in Paris zu nutzen, unterteilte der Architekt Alessandro Mosca den Raum horizontal und zog ein Zwischengeschoss ein, das über zwei verschiedene Treppenabschnitte zu erreichen ist. Die Treppe ist das zentrale Element des Lofts und führt zu dem ungewöhnlich aufgeteilten Obergeschoss. Auf einer Seite befinden sich das Schlafzimmer und das Studio, auf der anderen Seite das Badezimmer. Da die Gebäudestruktur sehr alt ist, wurde das Zwischengeschoss mit einer unabhängigen Struktur gestützt. Das Zwischengeschoss nimmt nicht die ganze Ebene ein, sondern es ist leicht zurückversetzt, so dass Licht durch die Fenster und Oberlichter einfallen kann. Für den Umbau wurden einfache, preisgünstige und widerstandsfähige Materialien verwendet und in der Dekoration wurde der Gegensatz zwischen den dominanten, blassen Farben der Wand und einzelnen, hellroten Elementen unterstrichen.

The configuration of the staircase sets up an interesting distribution of space and visually separates the areas that differentiate the kitchen and the living area.

La configuration de l'escalier crée une distribution intéressante de l'espace, instaurant une division visuelle et spatiale entre la cuisine et le salon

Durch die Gestaltung der Treppe entstand eine interessante Raumaufteilung. Die Treppe trennt visuell den Küchen- und Wohnzimmerbereich voneinander ab.

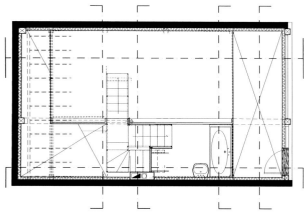

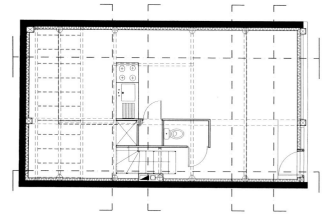

› First floor Premier étage Erstes Obergeschoss

› Ground floor Rez-de-chaussée Erdgeschoss

The mezzanine does not occupy the overall surface area but pulls back slightly to allow light to pour in through the windows and the skylights.

La mezzanine n'occupe pas toute la surface mais est légèrement en retrait pour permettre à la lumière naturelle de pénétrer à travers les fenêtres et les velux.

Das Zwischengeschoss nimmt nicht die ganze Ebene ein, sondern es ist leicht zurückgesetzt, so dass Licht durch die Fenster und Oberlichter einfallen kann.

Barcelona, Spain

Cortés Loft

These premises in Barcelona, formerly a textile warehouse, were converted by the prestigious designer Pepe Cortés into his own home. The existing height permitted the construction of a loft that includes a terrace with a garden and a swimming pool. The large windows on the upper level allow the entire space to be flooded with natural light. Areas are marked out by sliding doors, curtains and perforated partitions, which are translucent but can provide privacy when necessary. The project brings together a great variety of materials–either recycled from the original building, such as the iron in the column and wood in part of the structure, or new elements like marble, plaster painted in bright colors, aluminum and glass. Cortés personalized the settings with artworks created by friends, souvenirs from trips, and various well-known pieces of furniture of his own design.

Pepe Cortés, designer de renom, a transformé cet ancien entrepôt de textile de Barcelone, pour y élire domicile. La hauteur du bâtiment a permis de construire un loft avec une terrasse, un jardin et une piscine. Les larges baies vitrées de l'étage supérieur inondent l'espace de lumière naturelle. Portes coulissantes, rideaux et cloisons ajourés translucides délimitent les pièces, tout en assurant, le cas échéant, une certaine intimité. Le projet réunit une grande diversité de matériaux – certains récupérés de l'ancien bâtiment, à l'instar du fer dans les piliers et du bois dans certaines parties de la structure ou d'autres nouveaux éléments tels que le marbre, le plâtre peint dans des couleurs vives, l'aluminium et le verre. Pour personnaliser la construction, Cortés a ajouté des œuvres d'art créées par des amis, des souvenirs de voyage et plusieurs meubles design très connus, fruits de sa création.

Diese Räume in Barcelona liegen in einem ehemaligen Textilwarenhaus, das der bekannte Designer Pepe Cortés zu seiner eigenen Wohnung umbaute. Man konnte in den sehr hohen Räumen ein Loft mit angrenzenderTerrasse schaffen, auf der sich ein Garten und ein Swimmingpool befinden. Durch die großen Fenster auf der oberen Ebene dringt reichlich Tageslicht ein. Die verschiedenen Bereiche sind durch Schiebetüren, Vorhänge und lichtdurchlässige Raumteiler mit Öffnungen abgeteilt. Es kann Privatsphäre geschaffen werden, wenn es notwendig ist. Bei der Gestaltung wurden viele verschiedene Materialien eingesetzt, die wie das Eisen der Säulen und das Holz an Teilen der Struktur aus dem Originalgebäude stammen, oder neue Elemente wie Marmor, Gips in hellen Farben, Aluminium und Glas. Cortés dekorierte sein Zuhause sehr persönlich mit von Freunden gestalteten Kunstwerken, Reisesouvenirs und verschiedenen, bekannten Möbelstücken aus seiner eigenen Kollektion.

The numerous works of art reinforce the dynamic and colorful spirit that guided the design of all of the rooms in the residence.

Les nombreuses œuvres d'art exaltent le design dynamique et haut en couleurs qui caractérise toutes les pièces de la résidence.

Die zahlreichen Kunstwerke unterstreichen die dynamische und bunte Atmosphäre, die die Gestalter geschaffen haben.

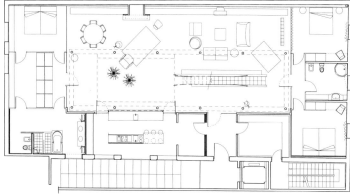

› Ground floor Rez-de-chaussée Erdgeschoss

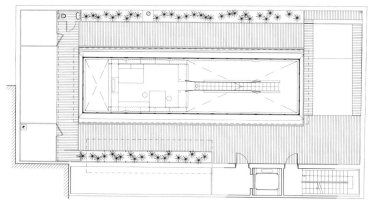

› First floor Premier étage Erstes Obergeschoss

The upper level boasts two magnificent terraces; the swimming pool and lush vegetation have turned it into an authentic urban oasis.

Le niveau supérieur se targue de deux superbes terrasses. La piscine et la végétation exubérante le métamorphosent en une véritable oasis en plein cœur de la ville.

Im Obergeschoss befinden sich zwei wundervolle Terrassen, der Swimmingpool und eine üppige Vegetation, eine wahre Stadtoase.

i/Chia Studio

Flower District Loft

New York, United States

The client of this New York loft wanted a design that would accommodate office work by day and large business events or intimate social gatherings by night. The open public areas are visually choreographed so that they can merge, compress, and expand, depending on the client's needs. Its "elasticity" allows it to expand for a large, crowded party or to contract into separate zones for the more intimate gatherings and events. A compact volume of private space contains a guest bedroom, gym, powder room, and two bathrooms, compressing the center of the public area into the kitchen, which becomes the focal point of the loft. Translucent screen doors mounted on aluminum frames allow the passage of light from the private core to the public areas. Their pattern, inspired by the traditional Indian jali, creates a shifting pattern of translucency, depending on the direction in which the light passes through the materials.

A la requête du client, ce loft de New York, conçu pour faire office de bureau pendant la journée, sert de salle de grandes réunions d'affaires ou de réceptions sociales plus intimes, le soir. Les espaces ouverts au public, selon une mise en scène visuelle, fusionnent, se compriment et s'élargissent au gré des besoins du client. Cette « élasticité » permet de moduler l'espace : l'élargir pour une grande réception ou le diviser en petites zones séparées pour les réunions ou évènements à caractère privé. Le volume d'une unité privée comprend une chambre d'invités, une salle de gymnastique, un boudoir et deux salles de bains, limitant le centre de la partie publique à la cuisine, le point de mire du loft. Des portes de verre translucides montées sur châssis d'aluminium laissent passer la lumière de la sphère privée aux zones publiques. Leurs motifs, inspirés du jali indien traditionnel, créent des jeux de lumière changeants, au gré des matériaux qu'elle traverse.

Für dieses Loft in New York wünschte sich der Kunde eine Gestaltung, die sich sowohl tagsüber beruflich als auch abends für Geschäftsveranstaltungen oder private Zusammenkünfte nutzen lässt. Die offenen Bereiche können visuell verändert werden, sie können nach Wunsch zusammengeschlossen, verkleinert und vergrößert werden. Diese „Elastizität" macht sowohl eine große, belebte Party als auch kleine Treffen und private Gespräche möglich. Ein kompaktes Volumen mit Privaträumen enthält ein Gästezimmer, einen Sportraum und zwei Badezimmer. Das Zentrum des öffentlichen Bereiches ist die Küche, die damit auch Mittelpunkt des Lofts ist. Lichtdurchlässige Türen auf Aluminiumrahmen lassen Helligkeit durch, die von den privaten Räume in die öffentlich genutzten dringt. Ihre Muster, inspiriert von dem traditionellen, indischen Jali, lassen wechselnde Lichtmuster entstehen, die sich verändern, wenn das Licht aus einer anderen Richtung durch die Materialien fällt.

The client wanted a design that would accommodate office work by day and large business events or intimate social gatherings by night.

Le client voulait un espace design qui puisse accueillir des bureaux pendant la journée et d'importantes réunions d'affaires ou de réceptions plus intimes le soir.

Der Kunde wünschte sich eine Raumgestaltung, die sowohl für die Büroarbeit tagsüber als auch für längere, geschäftliche Treffen oder private Zusammenkünfte an den Abenden geeignet ist.

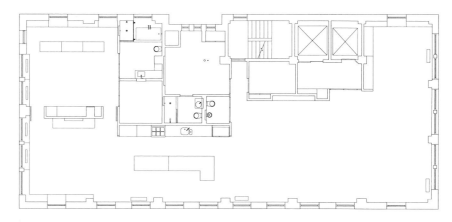

› Plan   Plan   Grundriss

The kitchen made of walnut and stainless steel becomes the focal point of the loft and takes advantage of the light coming in from the floor-to-ceiling windows.

La cuisine en noyer et acier inoxydable est le point de mire du loft. Elle bénéficie de la lumière qui arrive par les baies vitrées.

Die Küche aus Nussbaum und Edelstahl ist der Mittelpunkt des Loftes. Hier dringt das Licht, das durch das deckenhohe Fenster fällt, direkt ein.

Translucent screen doors mounted on aluminum frames allow light to pass from the private core to the public areas.

Des paravents translucides montés sur châssis d'aluminium permettent à la lumière d'aller des sphères privées aux zones publiques.

Lichtdurchlässige Türen auf Aluminiumrahmen lassen das Licht durch, das von den privaten Zimmern in die Räume mit öffentlicher Nutzung dringt.

The large windows and big mirrors, as well as the stone used for the surfaces, make the bathroom bright and welcoming.

Les grandes fenêtres et immenses miroirs alliés à la pierre des revêtements de surfaces agrandissent la salle de bains lumineuse et accueillante.

Die riesigen Fenster und großen Spiegel und die mit Naturstein verkleideten Wände schaffen eine helle und freundliche Atmosphäre im Badezimmer.

Rosenberg Residence
Résidence Rosenberg
Rosenberg Residenz

New York, United States

This residence, a multi-use project in an early-20th century commercial building, is spread over two 1,500 square-feet floors, converted into a living space during the 1980s. The two floors are vertically connected, with the interior renovated as an office, studio, and home for the art-loving occupant. From the outset, this special relationship between the two units played a prominent role, and the architects managed to develop a language that paradoxically joins both parts and makes them independent. On the upper floor, the home contains a living room, a kitchen, and two bedrooms. No partitions break up the exterior wall, which lets in abundant light from the north. The lower level, with its restored, sandblasted, concrete flooring cast with zinc, serves as both office and studio. The two levels are connected by a staircase that seems to have come straight from a ship and separates the work area and the living area on the upper floor.

Cette résidence, un projet polyvalent dans un bâtiment commercial du début du XXe siècle, d'une superficie au sol de 140 m², a été transformée en surface habitable dans les années 80. Les deux étages sont reliés verticalement. L'intérieur a été restauré en bureau, studio et logement pour un amoureux de l'art. Dés le départ, la relation particulière entre les deux unités a joué un rôle prépondérant, amenant les architectes à développer un langage paradoxal permettant de les joindre tout en les gardant indépendant. A l'étage supérieur, il y a un salon, une cuisine et deux chambres. Le mur extérieur n'est pas divisé et laisse pénétrer à flots la lumière du nord. Le niveau inférieur, au sol rénové en béton à jets de sable et zinc, sert à la fois de bureau et de studio. Les deux niveaux sont reliés par un escalier qui semble venir directement d'un bateau. Il sépare le salon du bureau, à l'étage supérieur.

Diese vielseitig genutzten Räume in einem Geschäftshaus aus dem frühen 20. Jh. sind 140 m² groß, und wurden 1980 in Wohnräume umgestaltet. Die beiden Etagen sind vertikal miteinander verbunden, und Büro, Atelier und das Heim des Bewohners wurden renoviert. Die besondere Beziehung zwischen den beiden Einheiten spielte von Anfang an eine wichtige Rolle, und dem Architekten gelang es, diese beiden Einheiten miteinander zu verbinden und voneinander unabhängig zu machen. Auf der oberen Etage befinden sich das Wohnzimmer, die Küche und zwei Schlafzimmer. Die äußere Wand wird nicht unterbrochen und es strömt viel Licht vom Norden ein. Das untere Stockwerk mit seinem restaurierten, sandgestrahltem Betonboden mit Zink dient sowohl als Büro als auch als Atelier. Die beiden Ebenen werden durch eine Treppe verbunden, die von einem Schiff zu stammen scheint, und die den Arbeitsbereich von dem Wohnbereich trennt.

Hatchway-like stairs connect the two levels and separate the work area from the private quarters on the upper floor.

Des escaliers, à l'instar d'écoutilles, relient les deux niveaux entre eux séparant l'espace bureau des quartiers privés à l'étage supérieur.

Treppen, die wie für Ladeluken gemaccht wirken, verbinden die beiden Ebenen und trennen den Arbeitsbereich vom Wohnbereich im Obergeschoss ab.

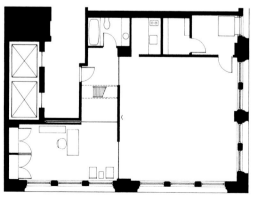

› Ground floor Rez-de-chaussée Erdgeschoss

› First floor Premier étage Erstes Obergeschoss

The furnishings in the kitchen and the bathroom are exclusively designed for the project.

Le mobilier de la cuisine et de la salle de bains a été conçu exclusivement pour ce projet.

Das Mobiliar der Küche und des Badezimmers wurde exklusiv für diese Räume entworfen.

Loft in Amsterdam
Loft à Amsterdam
Loft in Amsterdam

Amsterdam, Netherland

This fully restored loft space preserved its wooden beams and large façade windows by incorporating a central module that distributes the day and night areas. The central unit, whose walls stop short of the ceiling to maintain spatial fluidity, incorporates a seamless series of cupboards and drawers, one of which pulls into a dining table. On the façade side, the kitchen installations take advantage of the light and views. A sliding, translucent glass door leads on to the bedroom and beyond. The opposite side contains room for storage and also leads to the bedroom. It can be closed off by a series of sliding panels that hang from a railing. The bathroom is contained within the unit; its opaque glass panel above the bathtub acts as the kitchen wall on the other side. An opening was maintained above the bathroom to avoid humidity and to allow light to enter the space.

Ce loft entièrement restauré a gardé ses poutres de bois et ses grandes baies vitrées d'origine en intégrant un module central autour duquel s'articulent les parties jour et les parties nuits. Les murs de cet axe central ne vont pas jusqu'au plafond pour conserver la fluidité de l'espace. Toute une série de placards et tiroirs à bords lisses y sont encastrés, et l'un d'eux se transforme en table. Du côté de la façade, la cuisine bénéficie de la lumière et de la vue. Une cloison de verre translucide coulissante s'ouvre sur la chambre et au-delà, sur un espace rangement qui communique aussi avec elle. Cette partie peut être masquée par une série de cloisons coulissantes suspendues à un rail. Une salle de bains est aussi intégrée au module. Une cloison de verre opaque à côté de la baignoire fait aussi office de mur pour la cuisine située de l'autre côté. Au-dessus de la baignoire, il y a une ouverture contre l'humidité qui permet à la lumière de pénétrer l'espace.

In diesem renovierten Loft blieben die Holzbalken und die großen Fenster erhalten und es wurde ein zentrales Modul eingebaut, das die Bereiche für den Tag und die Nacht unterteilt. Diese zentrale Einheit, deren Wände nicht bis zur Decke reichen, um den Raum nicht zu unterbrechen, enthält eine nahtlose Reihe von Schränken und Schubladen, eine davon wird zum Esstisch. Die Arbeitsseite der Küche liegt bei den Fenstern, hell und mit Ausblick. Eine lichtdurchlässige Schiebetür aus Glas führt zum dem Schlafzimmer und weiter. Auf der anderen Seite gibt es Lagerraum und man gelangt ebenfalls zum Schlafzimmer. Dieses kann durch eine Reihe von gleitenden Paneelen geschlossen werden. Das Badezimmer befindet sich ebenfalls in dieser Einheit, das undurchsichtige Glaspaneel über der Badewanne ist gleichzeitig die Küchenwand. Eine Öffnung über dem Badezimmer sorgt für Licht und verhindert die Bildung von Feuchtigkeit.

The inserted central module distribute the day and night areas while maintaining the spatial fluidity of the whole space.

Le module central intégré distribue les aires de jour et de nuit tout en conservant la fluidité spatiale de l'espace entier.

Das eingefügte, zentrale Modul unterteilt die Bereiche in Zonen für tagsüber und nachts, ohne dabei die Kontinuität des gesamten Raumes zu unterbrechen.

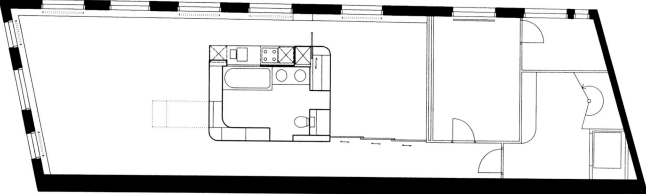

› Plan   Plan   Grundriss

The module contains storage space and can be closed off by a series of sliding panels that hang from a railing.

Le module offre un espace de rangement qui peut être fermé par une série de cloisons coulissantes suspendes à un rail.

In dem Modul ist Lagerplatz vorhanden und es kann mit einer Reihe von gleitenden Paneelen auf Schienen abgeschlossen werden.

An opening was maintained above the bathroom to avoid humidity and to allow light to enter the space.

L'ouverture maintenue au-dessus de la salle de bains permet d'éliminer l'humidité et d'inonder l'espace de lumière.

Eine Öffnung über dem Badezimmer sorgt für Licht und verhindert die Bildung von Feuchtigkeit.

Loft in an Attic
Loft dans un attique
Loft in einem Dachgeschoss

Madrid, Spain

This loft in a 150-year-old building in Madrid was transformed from a small space unsuitable for domestic purposes to a modern residence. To expand the useable floor space, the architect took advantage of the high ceilings and, in the tallest part of the space, under the sloping roof, he divided the area into two levels. The utmost care was taken to optimize the space, and the result is a playful exploration of the concept of a home that avoids traditional, rigid models and emphasizes functional flexibility. When the residents want to eat, the entire loft becomes a dining room; when they want to sit down, the entire space turns into a living room; and when they want to sleep, the entire apartment is a bedroom. Technical rigor and constructional precision were the essential tools for the successful completion of the project.

Situé dans un édifice madrilène vieux de 150 ans, ce loft, petit espace inadapté aux besoins d'une famille, a été restructuré en une résidence moderne. Pour augmenter l'espace utilitaire au sol, l'architecte a tiré parti de la hauteur de plafond : sous le toit en pente et au plus haut point, il a divisé l'espace en deux parties. L'espace a donc été optimalisé au maximum. Le résultat final est une maison conçue sous une approche ludique, loin des modèles traditionnels et rigides, exaltant ainsi la flexibilité fonctionnelle. A l'heure des repas, tout le loft devient salle à manger; lorsque les occupants veulent s'asseoir, l'espace entier se métamorphose en salon et à l'heure du coucher, l'ensemble de l'appartement se transforme en chambre à coucher. La réussite de ce projet repose sur la rigueur technique et la précision de construction.

Dieses Loft in einem 150 Jahre alten Gebäude in Madrid wurde von einem unbewohnbaren, kleinen Raum in eine moderne Wohnung umgebaut. Um mehr Platz zu schaffen, nutzte der Architekt die hohen Decken und zog im höchsten Teil unter dem geneigten Dach eine zweite Ebene ein. Ziel war es, den Raum optimal auszunutzen. So entstand die verspielte Interpretation einer Wohnung, in der traditionelle und steife Modelle vermieden und eine funktionelle Vielseitigkeit betont werden. Wenn die Bewohner essen möchten, wird das ganze Loft zum Esszimmer, möchten sie sich hinsetzen, wird alles zum Wohnzimmer, und möchten sie schlafen, ist die ganze Wohnung das Schlafzimmer. Das wurde mit sehr präzise eingesetzten Bautechniken erreicht.

The ingenious design has created a wooden terrace extending into the interior, producing a platform that can be used for sitting outdoors.

Fruit d'un design ingénieux, la terrasse extérieure se prolonge vers l'intérieur, créant une plate-forme qui peut être utilisée pour s'asseoir dehors.

Teil der interessanten Gestaltung ist eine Terrasse aus Holz, die sich nach innen erstreckt und eine Plattform bildet, auf der man draußen sitzen kann.

› Ground floor   Rez-de-chaussée   Erdgeschoss

› First floor   Premier étage   Erstes Obergeschoss

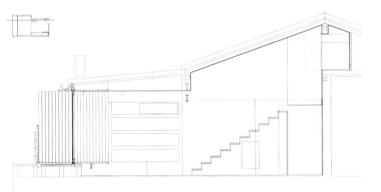

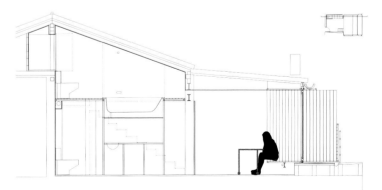

› Longitudinal sections   Sections longitudinales   Längsschnitte

313

House in Fukaya
Maison à Fukaya
Haus in Fukaya

Fukaya, Japan

This house is located in a site often described as a city suburb, due to its proximity to central Tokyo. As for the location, the architect Waro Kishi chose a closed configuration, while keeping an open interior space. The house has a rectangular layout, with the southern part containing the private elements, the garage and bedrooms, spread over two levels. The northern part, which is a half-level higher, contains the living and dining areas. A courtyard with a pool is located in the center of the building, connecting the southern and northern parts while also functioning as an exterior living room. By placing the horizontal stress on the exterior wall structure, the glass can be attached directly to two 4-inch posts, so that they stand free from both the sash windows and the wall structure. Factory materials and the visibility of the structural details give the building a real authentic character.

Cette maison se situe à un site souvent décrit comme les faubourgs de la cité, pour sa proximité du centre de Tokyo. L'architecte Waro Kishi a choisi de créer un ensemble fermé tout en gardant un espace intérieur ouvert. La maison est de conception rectangulaire, avec au sud les parties privées, le garage et les chambres réparties sur deux niveaux. La partie nord, constituée d'un demi-étage englobe, le salon et la salle à manger. La cour dotée d'une piscine, est située au centre de l'édifice. Trait d'union entre les parties sud et nord, elle fait office de salon extérieur. La tension horizontale étant placée sur l'ossature des murs extérieurs, le verre peut être directement fixé à deux tenants de 10 cm, devenant ainsi indépendants des deux fenêtres à guillotine et de l'ossature murale. Des matériaux d'usine et les détails apparents de la structure confèrent à l'édifice toute son authenticité.

Dieses Haus befindet sich in einer Gegend, die oft als Vorstadt bezeichnet wird, da sie so nah am Zentrum Tokios liegt. Aufgrund des Standortes wählte der Architekt Waro Kishi eine geschlossene Konfiguration, das Innere wurde jedoch offen gestaltet. Das Haus hat einen rechteckigen Grundriss. Im südlichen Teil befinden sich auf zwei Ebenen die privaten Räume, die Garage und die Schlafzimmer. Im nördlichen Teil, eine halbe Ebene höher, liegen Wohn- und Essbereich. Im Zentrum des Gebäudes befindet sich ein Hof mit einem Becken, der den südlichen und nördlichen Teil miteinander verbindet und gleichzeitig als ein Wohnzimmer im Freien dient.

Die horizontale Belastung liegt auf der äußeren Wandstruktur, so dass das Glas direkt an den 10 cm dicken Pfählen angebracht werden kann, und diese weder die Schiebefenster noch die Wandstruktur berühren. Das Gebäude wirkt durch den Einsatz von industriellen Materialien und den sichtbaren Strukturdetails sehr authentisch.

Full-height windows fill the rooms with natural light during the day and the white furniture accentuates the brightness of the space.

Des fenêtres tout en hauteur inondent les pièces de lumière du jour. Le mobilier blanc exalte la sensation d'espace.

Durch die deckenhohen Fenster fällt reichlich Tageslicht in die Räume und die weißen Möbel unterstreichen diese Helligkeit noch.

Industrial materials were used as an answer to the bleak surroundings, and the structural details are left visibly exposed.

L'emploi de matériaux industriels contraste avec la tristesse de l'environnement. Les détails de la structure sont parfaitement mis en relief.

Als Antwort auf die etwas triste Umgebung wurden industrielle Materialien eingesetzt, und die strukturellen Details nicht verborgen.

A pool has been inserted in the center of the courtyard to connect the southern and northern parts of the building.

Une piscine est intégrée au centre de l'atrium, à l'instar d'un trait d'union entre les parties sud et nord du bâtiment.

Ein Becken mitten im Hof verbindet die südlichen und nördlichen Gebäudeteile.

Dirty House
Maison Dirty
Dirty Haus

London, United Kingdom

The architect David Adjave, a graduate of the London's Royal College of Art who has worked with Eduardo Souto de Moura and David Chipperfield, is known as an architect with the vision of an artist. This project involved rebuilding a warehouse to create both a studio and a home. In order to begin with an open space, the structure had to be removed by building additional support into the interior walls of the studio spaces and thus taking the load off the residential floor. The main living zone occupies the ground-floor area, while the smaller spaces – the kitchen, bathroom, bedroom, and terraces facing south and west – are located around it. The centralized nature of this arrangement is given further emphasis by a skylight in the middle and the cantilevered roof. The skylight provides a level of natural light similar that that outside.

David Adjave, architecte diplômé du London's Royal College of Art, qui a travaillé avec Eduardo Souto de Moura et David Chipperfield, à la réputation d'être un architecte qui voit les choses avec un œil d'artiste. Ce projet englobe la reconstruction d'un entrepôt pour y créer un studio et une résidence. Pour ouvrir l'espace, il a fallu modifier la structure existante en insérant des supports supplémentaires dans les murs intérieurs du studio, soulageant ainsi le sol de la partie résidentielle. L'espace de vie principal occupe le rez-de-chaussée, alors que les autres - cuisine, salle de bains, chambre à coucher et terrasses face au sud et à l'ouest - s'articulent tout autour. Le caractère central de cette organisation est rehaussé par le puits de lumière au milieu et par le toit en encorbellement.

Der Architekt David Adjave, ausgebildet auf dem Londons Royal College of Art, hat bereits mit Eduardo Souto de Moura und David Chipperfield zusammengearbeitet. Er genießt einen guten Ruf als Architekt, der außerdem die Vision des Künstlers hat. Dieses Projekt umfasst den Umbau eines Lagerhauses zu einem Atelier und einer Wohnung. Zunächst wurden die Innenwände des Raumes, in dem das Atelier entstehen sollte, verstärkt, damit man Strukturelemente entfernen und an Platz gewinnen konnte. So wurde der Boden der Wohnbereiche entlastet. Die wichtigsten Wohnräume liegen im Erdgeschoss, umgeben von den kleineren Räume wie Küche, Bad, Schlafzimmer und den Terrassen nach Süden und Westen. Ein Oberlicht und das freitragende Dach unterstreichen die zentralisierte Gestaltung. Durch dieses Dachfenster wird der Raum taghell.

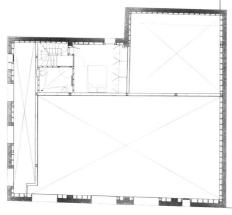

› Ground floor Rez-de-chaussée Erdgeschoss

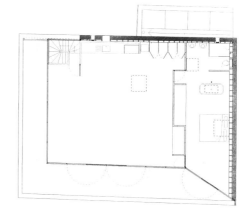

› First floor Premier étage Erstes Obergeschoss

322

The centralized layout is given further emphasis by a skylight in the middle of the cantilevered roof.

La conception centrale est accentuée par le velux installé au cœur du toit en cantilever.

Ein Oberlicht mitten in dem freitragenden Dach unterstreicht die zentralisierte Gestaltung.

Crepain Residence
Résidence Crepain
Crepain Residenz

Antwerp, Belgium

This project entailed the refurbishment of an industrial park in the center of Antwerp, Belgium. The architect converted an old warehouse into a living space and office for his own use. The residence combines domestic uses and the functions of a large exhibition space for an art collection. The main aims of the design were to restore the original building and respect its elements, and the success of this approach is evidenced by the effective preservation of the barrel roofs and the reopening of windows that had been boarded over. The home's living quarters are located on the top level, arranged around the splendid west-facing terrace. The kitchen and bathrooms are close to the elevator shaft, where all the electrical installations are assembled. Concrete was used for the remodeling throughout the residence, but was treated in different ways according to its function. The terrace, for example, was covered with aluminum and dark wood.

Ce projet a pour tâche de restaurer un parc industriel au centre d'Anvers, en Belgique. L'architecte a converti un ancien entrepôt en logement et bureau pour son usage personnel. La résidence réunit les services domestiques et les fonctions d'un vaste espace d'exposition pour une collection d'art. L'objectif principal du design est de restaurer le bâtiment d'origine et d'en respecter les éléments. La conservation des toits en berceau et la réouverture des fenêtres murées reflètent la réussite de cette approche. Les pièces à vivre se trouvent tout en haut, agencées autour d'une magnifique terrasse, face à l'est. La cuisine et les salles de bains sont proches de la cage de l'ascenseur où se trouve tout le système électrique. Le béton a été utilisé pour le remodelage de toute la résidence, traité différemment selon sa fonction : recouvert d'aluminium sur la terrasse, ou ailleurs, plaqué de bois sombre pour obtenir un fini plus chaleureux.

Dieses Projekt war Teil der Sanierung der Industrieanlagen im Zentrum von Antwerpen in Belgien. Der Architekt baute ein altes Warenhaus für sich selbst als Wohnung und Studio um. In dieser Wohnung wird gewohnt, aber es gibt auch einen großen Ausstellungsraum für Kunstwerke. Bei dem Umbau sollte vor allem das Originalgebäude restauriert und seine Elemente respektiert werden, was den Planern ausgezeichnet gelang. Das Dach blieb sehr gut erhalten und alle geschlossenen Fensteröffnungen wurden wieder geöffnet. Die Wohnräume im Obergeschoss umgeben eine wundervolle Terrasse nach Westen. Die Küche und Badezimmer liegen in der Nähe des Fahrstuhlschachtes, in dem alle elektrischen Installationen untergebracht sind. In allen Räumen wurde Beton verwendet, aber er wurde je nach Funktion anders behandelt. Auf der Terrasse wurde er mit Aluminium verkleidet und dort, wo ein wärmeres Material vonnöten war, mit dunklem Holz.

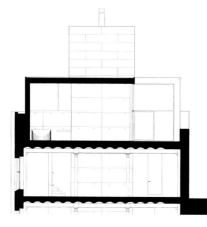

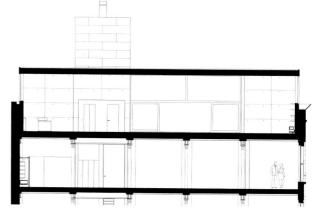

› Cross section   Section transversale   Querschnitt

› Longitudinal section   Section longitudinale   Längsschnitt

Loft on Rue Volta
Loft de la rue Volta
Loft in der Rue Volta

Paris, France

The architect Christophe Ponceau managed to convert these premises into a comfortable home, despite two major restrictions: on the one hand, the strong, reticulated, concrete structure that could not be modified in any way and, on the other, a ceiling that was two meters high at the beams and only two and a half meters high in the rest of the living space. The existing floor of granite slabs was totally removed and a fine layer of white cement with earth-colored flecks poured over the entire floor to enhance the feeling of spaciousness. In order to avoid breaking the stream of natural light coming in from outside, a window was placed in the partition between the living room and the studio. In this way, a visual relationship was also established between the rooms. Nearly all of the furniture was specially designed by the architect himself, creating a warm atmosphere.

L'architecte Christophe Ponceau a réussi à transformer ce bâtiment en un logement confortable, malgré deux contraintes majeures : d'un côté la structure massive et réticulée en béton, impossible à modifier, et de l'autre, un plafond de deux mètres de haut au niveau des poutres pour deux mètres et demi dans le reste de l'espace de vie. Pour rehausser la sensation d'espace, le sol pavé en granit préexistant a été éliminé et remplacé par une fine couche de ciment blanc, ponctuée de couleur terre. Afin de laisser passer la lumière naturelle venant de l'extérieur, une fenêtre a été installée dans la cloison séparant le salon du studio, créant ainsi un lien visuel entre les pièces. Tous les meubles ou presque, œuvres de l'architecte lui-même, créent une atmosphère chaleureuse.

Dem Architekten Christophe Ponceau gelang es, ein komfortables Heim zu schaffen, obwohl es dabei zwei Hindernisse gab. Zum einen war die starke Betonstruktur mit Netz, die nicht verändert werden konnte, und die Decke war an den Tragbalken nur zwei Meter hoch und im übrigen Wohnbereich zweieinhalb Meter. Der bereits vorhandene Boden aus Granitplatten wurde vollständig entfernt und eine Schicht weißen Zements mit erdfarbenen Flecken wurde auf den gesamten Fußboden aufgetragen, um das Gefühl von Weite zu verstärken. Ein Fenster in der Trennwand zwischen dem Wohnzimmer und dem Studio lässt das Tageslicht in den zweiten Raum strömen. So wurde eine visuelle Beziehung zwischen den beiden Räumen geschaffen. Der Architekt hat auch fast die ganzen Möbel entworfen, die eine sehr warme Atmosphäre schaffen.

The furniture design breaks up the pre-existing rigid structural system. Mobile modules, sliding doors and movable shelves make it possible to easily change the appearance of the residence.

Le design du mobilier rompt avec la rigidité du système structurel préexistant. Modules mobiles, portes coulissantes et étagères amovibles permettent de modifier facilement l'aspect de la résidence.

Durch die Gestaltung der Möbel wird das bereits vorhandene, steife Struktursystem unterbrochen. Bewegliche Module, Schiebetüren und bewegliche Regale machen es möglich, das Aussehen der Räume zu verändern.

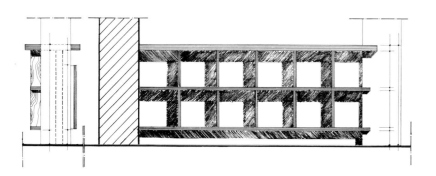

› Section Section Schnitt

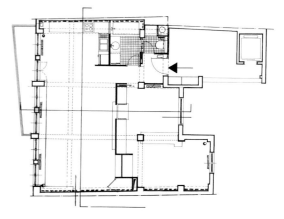

› Plan Plan Grundriss

Blue ceramic tiles are combined with white bathroom elements to create a cool but welcoming setting.

Céramiques bleues conjuguées aux éléments blancs de la salle de bains, créent une ambiance de fraîcheur accueillante.

Die blauen Keramikkacheln in Kombination mit den weißen Badezimmerelementen schaffe eine kühle, aber dennoch einladende Atmosphäre.

Flinders Lane

Melbourne, Australia

This former industrial space is defined by two main elements. The first is a multifunctional, free-standing wood-framed unit that encloses the sleeping area, provides storage space, serves as an auxiliary dining room, includes bookshelves, and is a sculptural element in itself. The second element is the set of patterns sandblasted into the original cement floor. The premises' industrial character was preserved by retaining features such as the original ventilation ducts, wrought-iron piping, and concrete floors. The bedroom unit is independent, touching neither the ceiling nor the lateral walls, and could easily be mistaken for a piece of furniture. While the wood and poly-carbonate unit separates the space into bedroom and living room, it also delimits the kitchen and leads on to the narrow entrance of the bedroom and bathroom.

Deux éléments essentiels caractérisent cet ancien bâtiment industriel. Le premier, une unité dotée d'une ossature de bois indépendante et polyvalente, accueille un dortoir et un espace de rangement qui peut servir de salle à manger annexe. Elle abrite des étagères de livres et ressemble à une sculpture. Le deuxième élément se définit par une série de motifs imprimés au jet de sable dans le sol en ciment. Le caractère industriel du site a été conservé en gardant certains éléments comme les gaines de ventilation d'origine, les conduites en fer forgé et les sols en béton. La chambre à coucher est une unité indépendante, ne touchant ni le plafond ni les murs latéraux et pourrait être facilement prise pour un meuble. Une unité en bois et poly carbonate scinde l'espace en chambre à coucher et salon et délimite aussi la cuisine. Elle mène également vers l'entrée étroite de la chambre à coucher et de la salle de bains.

Diese ehemalige Fabriketage zeichnet sich durch zwei Hauptelemente aus. Zum einen ist da die multifunktionelle, freistehende Einheit mit Holzrahmen um die Schlafzimmer, in der es auch Lagerplatz und Bücherregale gibt und die als behelfsmäßiges Esszimmer dient. Sie ist in sich selbst schon ein skulpturelles Element. Das zweite Element sind die sandgeblasenen Muster auf dem orgininalen Zementboden. Der industrielle Charakter des Gebäudes blieb erhalten, indem Elemente wie die einstigen Belüftungskanäle, Rohre aus gehämmerten Eisen und Betonböden gezeigt werden. Die Schlafzimmereinheit ist unabhängig und berührt weder die Decke noch die Seitenwände. Man könnte sie leicht für ein Möbelstück halten. Die Einheit aus Holz und Polycarbonat trennt den Schlaf- vom Wohnbereich, und sie begrenzt auch die Küche und führt zu dem engen Zugang zum Schlafzimmer und Bad.

The wood-framed, polycarbonate unit serves as a partition wall and allows light to flow through the whole area.

L'unité en poly carbonate, encadrée de bois, sert de cloison et permet à la lumière d'inonder toute la surface.

Die holzgerahmte Einheit aus Polycarbonat dient als Trennwand und lässt überall Licht durch.

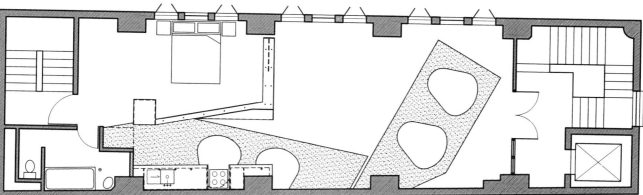

› Plan Plan Grundriss

Residence in Toronto
Résidence à Toronto
Residenz in Toronto

Toronto, Canada

This loft, located in an old industrial neighborhood, was originally divided into two but these have been fused to form a single cohesive space. The designers' aim was to create a space in which the original structure and the intervention's elements would complement each other. The old truss system was preserved and the floors and columns were newly installed to recover the original color and texture and to create a rustic effect. The housing was constructed using as base units some storage cabinets found in an old factory, some enormous refrigerator doors, and some recycled pieces from a cafeteria. To match these, the architects Cecconi Simone Inc. designed a kitchen counter, a bed with incorporated lighting, and a piece of furniture for the office. The windows were left untouched, since their large dimensions offered extraordinary ventilation and outstanding views of the city.

Ce loft, situé dans un ancien quartier industriel, était à l'origine scindé en deux parties, réunies désormais pour ne former qu'un seul espace. L'idée du designer était de créer un univers où la structure originale et les éléments nouveaux seraient complémentaires. Il a gardé l'ancienne ossature et rénové les sols et les colonnes en leur donnant l'ancienne couleur et texture pour créer un effet rustique. L'habitation a été construite en utilisant des armoires de rangement trouvées dans l'usine, d'énormes réfrigérateurs et d'objets recyclés de cafétéria. Pour les intégrer tous, les architectes Cecconi Simone s.a.r.l., ont dessiné le bar de la cuisine, un lit avec éclairage intégré et un meuble de bureau. Les fenêtres sont d'origine, leur taille imposante permettant une ventilation extraordinaire et offrant une superbe vue sur la ville.

Dieses Loft in einem alten Industrieviertel war einst in zwei Wohnungen unterteilt, aber es wurde zu einer zusammenhängenden Einheit umgebaut. Der Gestalter wollte innerhalb der Originalstruktur einen Raum schaffen, in dem die einzelnen, neu eingeführten Elemente einander ergänzen. Das alte Hängewerk blieb erhalten und die Fußböden und Säulen wurden neu konstruiert, um die ehemalige Farbe und Textur wieder herzustellen und eine rustikale Wirkung zu erzielen. Die Wohnung wurde mit einigen Grundeinheiten wie Lagerschränken aus einer alten Fabrik, riesigen Kühlschranktüren und einigen recycelten Stücken aus einer Cafeteria konstruiert. Zu diesem Stil passend entwarfen die Architekten Cecconi Simone Inc. eine Küchentheke, ein Bett mit integriertem Licht und ein Möbel für das Büro. Die Fenster blieben unverändert, da sie aufgrund ihrer Größe für eine ausgezeichnete Belüftung und einen wundervollen Blick über die Stadt sorgten.

The drapes, hanging from rods in the ceiling, can be moved to change the home's configuration or even arranged to create a separate room.

Les tentures, suspendues au plafond par des cordes, peuvent être déplacées pour moduler l'espace ou même créer une pièce séparée.

Die Vorhänge, die an Stangen an der Decke aufgehängt sind so dass die Aufteilung verändert wird. Sie können sogar so arrangiert werden, dass separate Räume entstehen.

› Plan Plan Grundriss

Loft in Sant Joan Despí
Loft à Sant Joan Despí
Loft in Sant Joan Despí

Sant Joan Despí, Spain

When the architect Agustí Costa set about refurbishing this studio under the roof of a detached house, he was confronted with a mixture of rustic furniture and disconnected structural elements that added up to a somewhat forbidding atmosphere. His project envisaged the creation of a living room that could be transformed into a bedroom and a work area suitable for all of the members of the family. Furthermore, the single space needed to provide sufficient privacy and isolation for different activities to be undertaken at the same time; to do this, a curved, false ceiling was installed, with openings at certain strategic points. All of the furnishings were painted the same grayish color, except for the red wall face that conceals the back of the chest of drawers, thus allowing it to assume more prominence. The lighting was integrated into the elements that structure the space.

Lorsque l'architecte Agustí Costa a entrepris la rénovation de ce studio sous les combles d'une maison individuelle, il a trouvé un mélange de meubles anciens et d'éléments structuraux dégageant une atmosphère légèrement austère. Il a conçu un salon modulable en chambre à coucher et une aire de travail convenant à tous les membres de la famille. Mais cet espace unique accueillant simultanément diverses activités, il était impératif de créer une certaine intimité et d'instaurer un système d'isolation. A cet effet, l'architecte a dessiné un faux plafond incurvé, doté d'ouvertures à certains points stratégiques. L'ensemble de l'ameublement se décline en gris à l'exception d'un pan de mur rouge abritant une commode, ainsi mise en valeur. L'éclairage est inséré dans les éléments structurant l'espace.

Als der Architekt Agustí Costa mit der Renovierung seines Studios im Dachgeschoss eines separaten Hauses begann, wurde er mit einer Mischung aus rustikalen Möbeln und unzusammenhängenden strukturellen Elementen konfrontiert, die eine nicht besonders angenehme Atmosphäre entstehen ließ. Es sollte ein Wohnzimmer geschaffen werden, das in ein Schlafzimmer verwandelt werden kann, und ein Arbeitsbereich für alle Familienmitglieder. Dieser einzige Raum sollte aber gleichzeitig genug Privatsphäre und eigenständige Bereiche bieten, dass verschiedene Aktivitäten gleichzeitig stattfinden konnten. Deshalb wurde eine gebogene, zweite Decke mit strategischen Öffnungen an bestimmten Stellen installiert. Das gesamte Mobiliar wurde in der gleichen gräulichen Farbe gestrichen. Nur die Wand, die die Hinterwand der Kommode verbirgt, ist rot und fällt dadurch ins Auge. Die Beleuchtung ist in die Strukturelemente integriert.

All of the construction details are well thought out and the design approach is unified. The result is a coherent atmosphere that affords a space where multiple activities may be carried out.

Tous les détails de la construction sont bien conçus, sous le sceau d'un design unifié. Il en résulte une atmosphère harmonieuse, dans un espace aux fonctions multiples.

Alle Konstruktionsdetail sind gut durchdacht, so dass der Gesamteindruck sehr einheitlich ist. Eine kohärente Wohnatmosphäre, die vielen Zwecken dient.

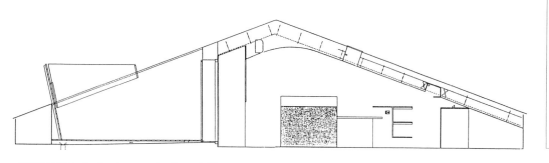

› Cross section Section transversale Querschnitt

› Plan Plan Grundriss

House and Garage
Maison et garage
Haus und Garage

A Coruña, Spain

This former warehouse was transformed into a single, two-story space with minimalist lines and strong colors. Different floor levels distribute the basic functions of the loft. The lower level contains the living and dining areas. The next level, distinguished by a taller ceiling, houses an integrated kitchen that can be closed off by a sliding opaque glass panel. The top level is accessed by a floating staircase that passes alongside a glass structure containing the main bathroom. The decorative surprise arrives in the living area, where the family car appears behind a glass wall that corresponds to the garage. In addition to transforming an industrial space into an innovative dwelling, the purpose of this project was to explore the social significance of the automobile as a functional and esthetic element in the home. Glass acts as a crucial component of this concept and design.

Cet ancien entrepôt a été réhabilité en un logement individuel à deux étages, aux lignes minimalistes ponctuées de couleurs vives. Les fonctions essentielles du loft sont réparties selon un système de différence de niveaux. Le niveau inférieur abrite le salon et la salle à manger. Au niveau suivant, défini par un plafond plus élevé, se trouve une cuisine intégrée qui peut disparaître derrière un panneau de verre opaque coulissant. L'accès au plus haut niveau se fait par un escalier flottant qui longe une structure en verre hébergeant la salle de bains principale. L'effet de surprise, côté décoration intérieure, est à son comble lorsqu'on entre dans la pièce à vivre où la voiture de famille apparaît derrière une cloison en verre, en guise de garage. Dans ce projet, à l'idée de transformer un espace industriel en une résidence originale, s'ajoute l'étude de l'impact social de l'automobile. Ici, le verre joue un rôle déterminant dans la conception et le design.

Diese ehemalige Lagerhalle wurde zu einem zweistöckigen Raum mit minimalistischen Linien und starken Farben umgestaltet. Die Grundfunktionen des Wohnens verteilen sich auf verschiedene Ebenen. Auf der unteren Ebene befinden sich die Wohn- und Essbereiche. Auf der nächsten Ebene mit sehr hoher Decke liegt die integrierte Küche, die durch eine Schiebetür mit opaker Glasplatte geschlossen werden kann. Die oberste Etage erreicht man über eine hängende Treppe entlang der Glasstruktur, in der sich das Hauptbadezimmer befindet. Eine überraschende Dekoration findet man im Wohnbereich. Von dort aus sieht man durch eine Glaswand das Auto in der Garage. In diesem Projekt wollte man auch die soziale Bedeutung des Autos als ein funktionelles und ästhetisches Element in einem Haus zeigen. Glas ist die wichtigste Komponente bei diesem Konzept und Design.

Materials like the red rubber floor in the living room define the boundaries between the different areas.

Des matériaux, à l'instar du linoléum rouge sur le sol du salon, délimitent les différents espaces.

Materialien wie der rote Kautschukbelag des Fußbodens im Wohnzimmer definieren die Grenzen zwischen den verschiedenen Bereichen.

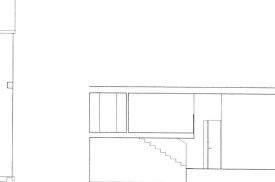

› Plan Plan Grundriss

› Sections Sections Schnitte

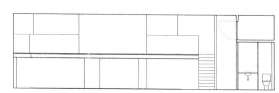

On the upper level, the floor was fitted out with natural coconut fiber, which adds warmth to the private space.

Le sol du niveau supérieur est revêtu de fibre naturelle de coco, conférant aux sphères privées une note chaude.

Auf der oberen Etage ist der Fußboden mit natürlicher Kokosfaser belegt, was die privaten Räume sehr warm und einladend wirken lässt.

Davol Loft

New York, United States

Located in a former warehouse in downtown Manhattan's old industrial area, this project began with an empty rectangular box, characterized by the typical attributes of a loft: columns down the center, enormous windows, and a high ceiling. This distinctive spatial configuration presented a challenge if living space and a fully operational work area were to be integrated. The clients, two journalists, needed separate bedrooms with adjacent bathrooms, a kitchen, a small storage area, a large, open living room, and a flexible work area for each of them. The service areas were placed against the windowless north and south walls but not totally separated from the rest of the loft visually, as if they were modules inserted into a container. Their walls do not reach the ceiling and iridescent materials are used to create magnificent reflective patterns that accentuate the lightness of the components.

Située dans un vieil entrepôt de l'ancienne zone industrielle du centre de Manhattan, ce projet a commencé par une boite rectangulaire vide, dotée des caractéristiques propres au loft : colonnes au centre, immenses fenêtres et plafond très haut. Cette configuration spatiale singulière présentait un véritable défi quant à l'intégration d'un espace salon et d'une aire de travail parfaitement opérationnelle. Les clients, deux journalistes, voulaient deux chambres séparées dotées de salles de bains contiguës, une cuisine, une petite zone de rangement, un vaste salon ouvert et une aire de travail modulable pour chacun des deux. Les zones de services ont été placées contre les murs nord et sud, dépourvus de fenêtres. Mais elles ne sont pas entièrement séparées du loft sur le plan visuel, à l'instar de modules intégrés à un container. Les murs ne vont pas jusqu'au plafond et des matériaux chatoyants créent de magnifiques motifs qui miroitent, exaltant la légèreté des éléments.

Dieses Loft in einer ehemaligen Lagerhalle im Industriegebiet von Downtown Manhattan war zunächst ein leerer, rechteckiger Kasten mit den typischen Kennzeichen einer Fabriketage, Säulen in der Mitte, riesige Fenster und eine hohe Decke. Dieser Raum stellte eine Herausforderung dar, da man ein Wohnzimmer und einen voll funktionierenden Arbeitsbereich integrieren wollte. Die Kunden, zwei Journalisten, benötigten zwei getrennte Schlafzimmer mit einem anliegenden Badezimmer, eine Küche, einen kleinen Lagerraum, ein offenes Wohnzimmer und zwei flexible Arbeitsbereiche. Küche und Bad befinden sich an den fensterlosen Nord- und Südwänden, sind aber visuell nicht vollständig vom Rest des Lofts abgetrennt, als ob sie Module in einem Container wären. Die Wände dieser Räume reichen nicht bis zur Decke. Durch schillernde Materialien entstehen wundervolle Lichtmuster, die die Leichtigkeit und Farbigkeit der eingesetzten Elemente unterstreichen.

The finishing produces a pattern of colors, reflections, and transparencies. The extraordinary impact of this setting is the result of intense experimentation with the materials.

La finition offre une gamme de couleurs, de reflets et de transparences. L'impact extraordinaire de cet agencement résulte d'une étude intense des matériaux.

Durch die Verwendung der Oberflächenmaterialien entstehen Muster aus Farben, Reflexen und Transparenzen. Die außerordentliche Wirkung dieser Wohnumgebung entstand durch ein intensives Experimentieren mit den Materialien.

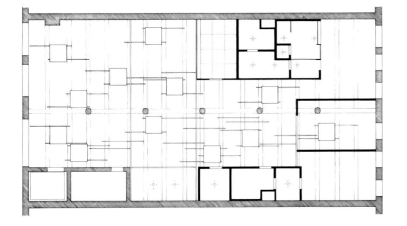
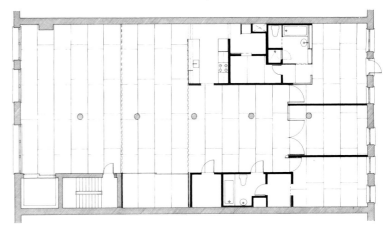

› Plans Plans Grundrisse

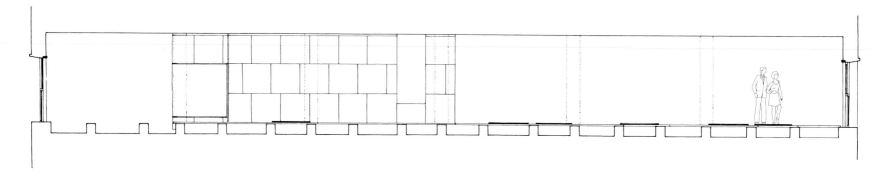

› Section Section Schnitt

This large, multi-use space must meet certain acoustic requirements because the clients often use it to rehearse.

Ce vaste espace polyvalent, souvent utilisé par les clients pour répéter, doit donc remplir certaines conditions au niveau de l'acoustique.

Dieser große, multifunktionelle Raum musste bestimme akustische Voraussetzungen erfüllen, da die Kunden ihn oft als Proberaum benutzen.

Some of the partitions are mobile, making it easy to redistribute the space inside the apartment. The panels' translucency sets up distinctive spatial relationships and avoids any permanent compartmentalization.

Certaines cloisons sont mobiles, permettant de moduler facilement l'appartement. En évitant un cloisonnement permanent, la translucidité des panneaux crée une relation spatiale différente.

Manche der Raumteiler sind beweglich, so dass die Aufteilung der Räume sehr leicht zu verändern ist. Durch die Lichtdurchlässigkeit der Paneele entstehen charakteristische räumliche Beziehungen und eine permanente Aufteilung wird vermieden.

The walls of the bathrooms do not reach the ceiling and iridescent materials are used, creating magnificent reflecting patterns that accentuate the components' lightness and colorfulness.

Les murs de la salle de bains n'atteignent pas le plafond et les matériaux chatoyants utilisés créent des motifs et reflets magnifiques qui rehaussent la légèreté des éléments hauts en couleurs.

Die Wände des Badezimmers reichen nicht bis zur Decke. Durch schillernde Materialien entstehen wundervolle Lichtmuster, die die Leichtigkeit und Farbigkeit der eingesetzten Elemente unterstreichen.

Tank modules
Modules base de réservoirs
Tankmodule

New York, United States

Located in what was previously the fourth floor of a parking lot in New York´s West Village, this is an excellent example of a project in which the term "loft" takes on a meaningful definition. The main condition was a separation of private and public areas that would refer to the location's industrial origins. Its high ceilings and regular shape led to the idea of inserting two gas tanks inside the space and turning them into bedroom and bathroom pods. The tanks contain the most intimate rooms of the residence, leaving the rest of the space free for the living area and kitchen. One of the modules, comprising two sleeping pods, is situated horizontally above the dining table and looks out over the living room and façade windows. The second tank, placed vertically from floor to ceiling, contains two bathrooms – one on top of the other. The lighting, the red furniture, and the blue floor add color that contrasts with the dominant gray tones.

Situé à New York, au quatrième étage d'un ancien parking du West Village, ce projet est l'exemple parfait du concept de « loft ». L'idée maîtresse était de créer une séparation entre le domaine privé et public rappelant l'origine industrielle du site. La hauteur des plafonds et la régularité de la forme ont donné l'idée d'intégrer à l'espace intérieur deux réservoirs à gaz et de les transformer en chambre à coucher et en salle de bains. Les sphères privées de la résidence sont installées dans ces réservoirs, libérant l'espace restant pour les pièces à vivre et la cuisine. L'un des modules contenant deux chambres, est à l'horizontale au-dessus de la table et surplombe le salon et les fenêtres de façade. Le deuxième réservoir, à la verticale et tout en hauteur, abrite deux salles de bains - l'une au-dessus de l'autre. L'éclairage, le rouge des meubles et le bleu du sol sont autant de touches de couleurs qui tranchent sur la dominante grise de l'ensemble.

Dieses im einstigen vierten Stock eines Parkhauses in der West Village in New York gelegene Loft ist ein ausgezeichnetes Beispiel für ein Projekt, bei dem der Begriff "Loft" an neuer Bedeutung gewinnt. Die wichtigste Planungsvorgabe war die Trennung der privaten und öffentlichen Bereiche, die an den industriellen Ursprung erinnern sollten. Die hohe Decke und die gleichmäßige Form brachten die Gestalter auf die Idee, zwei Gastanks in den Raum einzuführen und für das Schlaf- und Badezimmer zu benutzen. Wohn- und Küchenbereich blieben offen. Eines der Module bestehend aus zwei Schlafzonen befindet sich horizontal über dem Esstisch, so dass man über das Wohnzimmer und zum Fenster blickt. Der zweite Tank ist vertikal vom Boden zur Decke platziert und enthält zwei Bäder, die übereinander angeordnet sind. Die Beleuchtung, die roten Möbel und der blaue Fußboden setzen Farbtupfer in die von Grautönen dominierte Umgebung.

The insertion of gas tanks into a living space was a clever adaptation of industrial equipment to domestic use.

L'insertion de cuves de gaz à l'espace de vie est une façon judicieuse d'adapter le matériel industriel à l'usage domestique.

Das Einfügen der Gastanks in eine lebende Umgebung stellt eine intelligente Verwendung von industriellen Gegenständen im Wohnbereich dar.

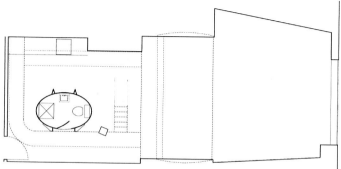

› **Ground floor** Rez-de-chaussée Erdgeschoss

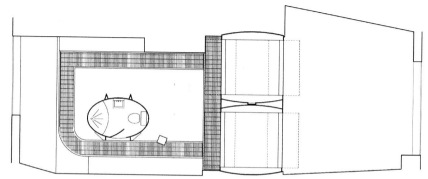

› **First floor** Premier étage Erstes Obergeschoss

Steel and Glass
Acier et verre
Stahl und Glas

Toronto, Canada

To renovate this loft, the architect Johnson Chou began by removing all non-structural walls and introducing a large sandblasted screen to divide the main space. In addition, he layered the space with sliding partitions, such as the stainless-steel panel that separates the bedroom from the living area. In the bedroom, an aluminum-clad king-size bed cantilevered from the wall floats in front of floor-to-ceiling aluminum closets spanning the length of the room. The platform containing the bathroom areas is clad in blue-green slate and distinguished by a sculptural, free-standing stainless-steel vanity that heralds the passage into the washing areas. A massive white column contrasts with the smoothness of the steel and glass, whose constant presence lend a certain depth and warmth despite their cool starkness. A strip of clear glass along the bathroom door indulges the voyeur with a view of the sunken slate bathtub from the living area.

Pour rénover ce loft, l'architecte Johnson Chou a commencé par ôter tous les murs non porteurs et a installé un grand écran poli au jet de sable pour diviser l'espace principal. A cela s'ajoutent des cloisons coulissantes qui scandent l'espace, comme le panneau en acier séparant la chambre de la pièce à vivre. Un immense lit recouvert d'aluminium, posé en cantilever sur le mur, flotte devant des armoires d'aluminium couvrant toute la largeur et la hauteur de la chambre. La plate-forme, hébergeant l'espace salle de bains, est recouverte d'ardoise bleu-vert et mise en valeur par un plan de toilettes en inox, auto portante et sculpturale, en prélude à la salle d'eau. Une colonne blanche et massive tranche avec la délicatesse de l'acier et du verre dont l'omniprésence confère profondeur et chaleur malgré leur froide sobriété. Un filet de verre court le long de la porte de la salle de bains et permet un regard indiscret, depuis le salon, sur l'élégante baignoire installée au raz du sol.

Zur Umgestaltung dieses Lofts ließ der Architekt Johnson Chou zunächst alle nicht tragenden Wände entfernen und unterteilte den Raum durch einen großen, sandgestrahlten Schirm. Außerdem wurden gleitende Raumteiler wie die Edelstahlplatten eingesetzt, die das Schlafzimmer vom Wohnzimmer trennen. Im Schlafzimmer schwebt ein freitragendes, riesiges Bett vor den deckenhohen Aluminiumschränken, die eine Seite des Raumes einnehmen. Die Plattform des Badezimmerbereiches ist mit blaugrünem Schiefer verkleidet. Der aussergewöhnliche freistehende Toilettentisch aus Edelstahl, steht am Übergang zum Waschbereich. Eine massive weiße Säule bildet einen Gegensatz zu dem glatten Stahl und Glas, die trotz ihrer Steife eine gewisse Tiefe und Wärme ausstrahlen. An der Badezimmertür befindet sich ein Glasstreifen, durch den man vom Wohnzimmer aus einen Blick auf die eingelassene Badewanne aus Schiefer erhaschen kann.

The electrical system provides maximum flexibility in the lighting while also contributing to the fluidity of the space.

Le système électrique permet de moduler au maximum l'éclairage tout en contribuant à la fluidité de l'espace.

Durch ein elektrisches System wurde eine sehr flexible Beleuchtung erzielt, durch die der Raum viel fließender wirkt.

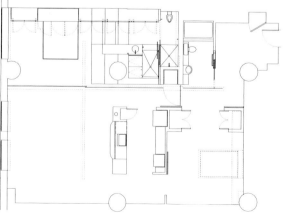

› Plan Plan Grundriss

In the bedroom, an aluminum-clad king-size bed cantilevered from the wall floats in front of an expanse of floor-to-ceiling aluminum closets that span the length of the room.

Dans la chambre, un immense lit recouvert d'aluminium, posé en cantilever sur le mur, flotte devant les armoires d'aluminium qui couvrent toute la largeur et la hauteur de la pièce.

Im Schlafzimmer entspringt ein riesiges, mit Aluminium beschlagenes Bett freitragend der Wand und scheint vor den vom Boden bis zur Decke reichenden Wandschränken, die die gesamte Länge des Raumes einnehmen, zu schweben.

The materials used for the bathroom elements are characterized by their purity and simplicity.

Les matériaux définissant les éléments de la salle de bains sont empreints de pureté et de simplicité.

Im Badezimmer wurden sehr einfache und reine Materialien eingesetzt.

The sunken bathtub is glimpsed from the living area through a 10-inch strip of clear glass running along the bathroom door.

Une bande de verre de 25 cm, le long de la porte de la salle de bains, permet un regard indiscret depuis le salon.

Vom Wohnbereich aus erhascht man durch den zehn Zentimeter breiten, durchsichtigen Glasstreifen an der Badezimmertür einen Blick auf die eingelassene Badewanne.

Photo Credits   Crédits photographiques   Fotonachweis

010-019	Andrea Martiradonna	210-217	Andrea Martiradonna
020-025	Juan Rodríguez	218-223	Catherine Tighe
026-033	Paul Warchol	224-229	Pascal Maréchaux
034-045	Matteo Piazza	230-237	Catherine Tighe
046-051	Jordi Miralles	238-243	Gunnar Knechtel
052-059	Jose Luis Hausmann	244-249	Andrea Martiradonna
060-067	Andrea Martiradonna	250-253	Eduard Hueber
068-073	Björg Photography	254-259	Eduard Hueber
074-079	Eduard Hueber	260-265	Peter Warren
080-085	David M. Joseph	266-271	Hervé Abbadie
086-093	Roberto Pierucci	272-277	Hervé Abbadie
094-099	Andreas Wagner, Margherita Spiluttini	278-285	Eugeni Pons
100-103	Hervé Abbadie	286-293	Joshua McHugh
104-109	Eduard Hueber	294-299	Christopher Wesnofske
110-115	Matteo Piazza	300-307	Christian Richters
116-121	Hervé Abbadie	308-313	Luis Asín
122-127	Fabien Baron	314-319	Hiroyuki Hirai
128-133	Daniel Moulinet	320-323	Lyndon Douglas
134-143	Virginia del Giudice	324-327	Jan Verlinde, Ludo Nöel
144-149	Dennis Gilbert/View	328-333	Alejandro Bahamón
150-157	Nick Hufton/View	334-339	Shannon Mcrath
158-165	Catherine Tighe	340-345	Joy von Tiedemann
166-171	Jean Villain	346-351	David Cardelús
172-179	Christian Richters	352-357	Alberto Peris Caminero
180-187	Andrea Martiradonna	358-367	Michael Moran
188-195	Hervé Abbadie	368-373	Paul Warchol
196-203	Andrea Martiradonna	374-381	Volker Seding Photography
204-209	Hervé Abbadie		